Old School Simple

A simple guide for small business owners struggling to keep up with the pace of technology

By
Krish Sailam

Dedication

To my wife,
Ikdienas es atrast jaunu iemesls iemīlēties ar jums, bet šodien ir vissvarīgākais.

And to my Father,
Thanks for reminding me to finish what I started.

Introduction - Can I let technology pass me by?

Since the mid-1990s, friends and family have asked me about various types of new technology, questions as simple as "What are DVDs?" to "What is the Internet?"

I distinctly remember my dad asking me, "What is the difference between the Internet and the World Wide Web?" Most people use these terms interchangeably, but there are differences.

People inherently have a limit to how much technology they can consume. This limit might be due to time, perhaps money, lack of a foundation, or just lack of desire. Everyone has a limit, even the twenty-year-old hipster who thinks he or she is on the bleeding edge.

For instance, your grandfather probably doesn't have a need to see what the top ten blogs are saying about a particular issue. He may be more than happy with the level of news in that old yet reliable piece of technology called a newspaper.

Given that all technology that comes out these days is a "game changer" and "magical," are we really missing anything? Can we effectively desensitize ourselves to all the noise and still be good at running a business? Why should we learn the newest magical technology if the next thing is going to be even better?

That is a major question: Why learn something new?

Humans are pack animals; we have a need to be around other humans. This pack mentality usually appears in high school with the definition of the popular kids, the jocks, the nerds, etc. People realize they can't hang out with everyone all the time, so they create subgroups of people they look like or want to be like.

Ah, an underlying desire to be popular or part of the in-crowd.

In the animal world, the strongest group tends to survive. We mimic this power contest by evaluating social influence and power as the ability to survive.

Back to that question, why learn something new? My take as an observer and amateur cultural anthropologist is that we learn it so we can communicate with the in-crowd. After all, they are "in" something, and I at least want to see what is there. For me to see that, I have to figure out how I can get on the in-crowd's system, their playing field, and their team. Some take it even further, thinking, "Once I am on their field, how can I become the cool one and displace the current leader?"

In today's world, our technology not only evolves quickly, but we get to see others enjoy and gain status by getting the right technology first.

Exhibit 1. Anders Schobel, one of the first iPad buyers in 2010.

If you didn't get the cool new technology first, you feel stressed. You now have to catch up. The in-crowd left without you again.

Remember Betamax versus VHS?

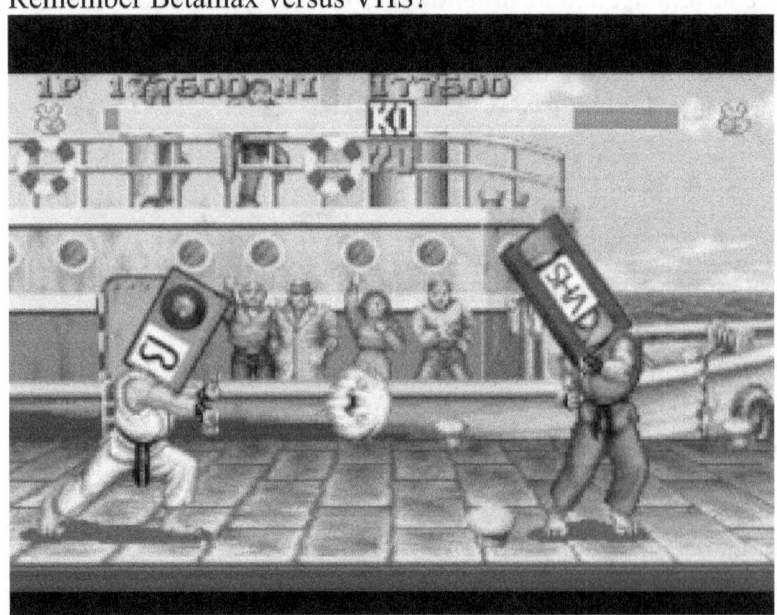

Exhibit 2. Betamax versus VHS.
http://mroche.umwblogs.org/vhs-vs-betamax/

People started asking me about technology slightly before I became a teenager.

Imagine, a forty-five-year-old asking a twelve-year-old, "Hey, what is cool these days?"

I still get questions from people all the time asking me to explain how they can market on Facebook or Google AdWords, etc. I used to take time to explain it to them without asking any questions first.

Then it all dawned on me. I was asking these people to invest in something that changes daily, may not be relevant to them, and is expensive. On top of that, they had no time to monitor these systems.

I'd just become a really bad investment advisor. I was telling people to throw money out the window, and I wasn't providing them any tools for long-term success.

But they were thankful for the advice and left the room filled with hope about all the new things they could do with this technology.

You know what happened nine times out of ten? They tried it for about a day and then gave up. Worse, they lost their hard-earned money.

What happened?

They had too many options. When they got into it by themselves, they were overwhelmed. They had no idea where to start. They frantically searched for the instruction manual, a training guide, advice, the help section, or a support area. Anything.

Even worse, they weren't even sure what they were aiming for. They had no goal.

This insight started to reveal a larger issue in American society. We were and still are being conditioned to think that we must move faster and jump to the newest thing every time. This reminds me of a quote from a couple that had been married over 60 years, when asked how they stayed together so long, the wife answered "we were born in a time when if something was broken we would fix it, not throw it away..." With this constant jumping from one technology to another, we are moving so fast, we don't have time to establish a goal or take a moment to reflect on our decisions. We jump aimlessly and hope for the best every time. We also ignore a lot of value in our current assets.

All these new ideas about how to make money and grow a business through technology but nothing was sticking. I started to think of this as the "lottery syndrome." You spend $1.00 to see if you can win $200 million. The reality is that your odds of winning are so low, you'd be better off just keeping your dollar and coming out on top for the day.

Another way of putting this is to say if you had $1000 a month to buy better quality ingredients for your deli, versus $1000 to spend on technology that had no return, which one would you choose as a business owner?

The answer is easy, but somehow, we as business owners tend to choose the riskier investment time and time again.

Hold that thought.

I want to show you how the simple stuff is actually the most exciting and how the risky stuff is not worth your time. Best of all, it is the stuff you know how to do really well, and it is the original reason you went into business. I want you to break that dangerous cycle of jumping without a goal or purpose. I want you to rebuild the mental conditioning you have to say it is ok to sometimes let technology pass you by and allow your business to avoid haphazard decisions.

I think I frustrated a lot of people by explaining to them all these new ways of advertising online. For that I apologize. This book, in a way, is my attempt to make up for all of that frustration.

The tips and advice that is in this book is based on primary research, talking to a slew of small business owners, and personal experiences of how I ran my small businesses. I won't lie to you; I had my first company when I was 15 and I ran into the ground within a few months. Reflecting back on the past, I realized I had to be much more specific about my short terms goals to achieve my long term goals. I couldn't be a millionaire overnight, I had to first make $1. Later on in life I was part of the internet marketing boom in San Francisco. I gained a great deal of experience and insight into what people do online and how they perceive brands. This knowledge was based on millions of dollars of advertising campaigns targeting all types of races, genders, ages, and education levels. Being able to spend over a million dollars a month on an ad campaign was a lot of fun, and it wasn't nearly as stressful as spending $100 of my own money promoting a small business idea. With the larger ad budgets, there was room for error but more importantly the knowledge came in buckets not drops. Realizing that the majority of small businesses in America don't have very large advertising budgets, I knew there was a need to help all small businesses. The holy trinity of small business quickly became apparent, Customers, Time & Money. You never have enough of any of those!

In this book, I will show you how to figure out if a new technology is for you and how to make the most of the best technology you have already. If you do decide that you need a new piece of technology, I will walk you through the process of finding an amazing team, measuring progress, and getting your intended results. All of my recommendations are based on the premise that you need more customers, you don't have a lot of time, and money can't be wasted in your company.

It is a simple, three-step process:

- Ask – if the technology is relevant to your business.
- Define - a goal.
- Measure – the progress against the goal.

If for some reason you can't accomplish step two or three, you've solved your problem already! You can keep it simple and focus on your core product or service. Hallelujah!

The three-step formula is simple, but I want to walk you through each step so you are able to adapt it to your business, easily replicate it, and eventually master it.

The holy trinity of customers, money and time are challenges that you as a business owner must overcome. The Ask-Define-Measure process is a way for you to effectively get past those challenges and continue to see success in your business.

If you are a small business owner daunted by technology, please keep reading. I promise to keep things simple and give you plenty of guides along the way. Since technology is always changing, I encourage you to visit my website for updated information and to download the guides that you find in this book.

OldSchoolSimple.com

Section 1 - ASK

Chapter 1 -Where Do You Start?

The first step towards getting somewhere is to decide that you are not going to stay where you are. —Unknown

Before doling out advice, I need to know a little about you. More importantly, I want you to say it to yourself.

Often, I find people think they are in one business, but their customers think they are in a totally different business. This particular exercise helps identify if your business has lost focus or if you are being held back from truly achieving your vision. For the purposes of this book, my goal is to help you align your real business with your technology. To do this effectively, I need to know a few different aspects of your business. We will cover the following aspects:

- Your traits as an owner/manager – how you adapt and lead, also how you perceive technology
- Your core business model – how you make money
- Your marketing strategy – how you approach marketing and what you have done in the past
- Your technology goals – what is your technology supposed to do for you

Don't worry about having all of these answers right away, each chapter will help you identify where you are, where you want to go, and how you can get there.

The owner's mindset

The owner of any small business is the greatest asset and greatest liability. As owners, we lead the charge on initiatives that we feel confident in and we often do not trust our team to help fill in the gaps. If you look at small businesses over time, they usually reflect what the owner is strong at, not necessarily what the team is strong at. Lets say we have a local deli started by one man 20 years ago, his passion was bread and cured meats. He built his reputation and his business by making amazing sandwiches. He never tried to franchise, he never focused on online ordering, he never did TV commercials, and he never really grew past his loyal neighborhood. His business was a pure reflection of him exploiting one skill, but not really bringing in other team members to help him on other fronts.

The motivations behind this are sometimes fear, sometimes not caring, sometimes just not knowing where to start. Each person has their own reason, which leads me to how we as small business owners perceive and approach technology. The reason why I am focusing on technology here is two fold, it is the one I personally know best, and it is the one where I see a lot of small business owners get scammed.

This exercise is about identifying where you are in the technology adoption cycle. The technology adoption cycle is not only how you learn about technology, but it also covers how you incorporate it and embrace it. Keep in mind that most people don't embrace it, in fact most people are scared of technology. For me to help you keep your life simple and your business even more simple, I need you to be honest here with how you view technology.

In this exercise we will try to define your awareness level and comfort level with technology. Awareness in this instance is just how much you might have heard of a particular technology. Awareness also relates to your grasp of that technology. Some people may be aware of Twitter but are not sure how it works or even what it does. I would say this is "Aware" in the chart below.

Your comfort level is an emotional response or gut feeling you get when you hear about a particular technology. Most people ignore these responses and think they are ok with trying something. But if you are scared, take a moment to figure out what is scaring you about the technology. Is it because it is complicated, is it because it is expensive, or is it because you feel left behind? There are dozens of reasons, but the thing to focus on is how you as a business owner can get past your fear. This may involve other business owners, customers or consultants offering advice, however, it will ultimately be up to you to make a decision that is aligned with your core business goals.

Level	Awareness Level	Comfort Level
1	Unaware	Not Scared
2	Aware	Scared
3	Aware and Indecisive	Scared
4	Aware and Decisive	Not Scared
5	Aware & Decisive & Able to Replicate	Confident

Exhibit 3- Old School Simple Technology Awareness and Comfort Levels

Most people are in level one, unaware and not scared. This is blissful ignorance. Once you get to level two, aware and scared, then all hell breaks loose. By level five, things have calmed down again and technology has been successfully integrated into your business.

Another way to portray this cycle is the following:

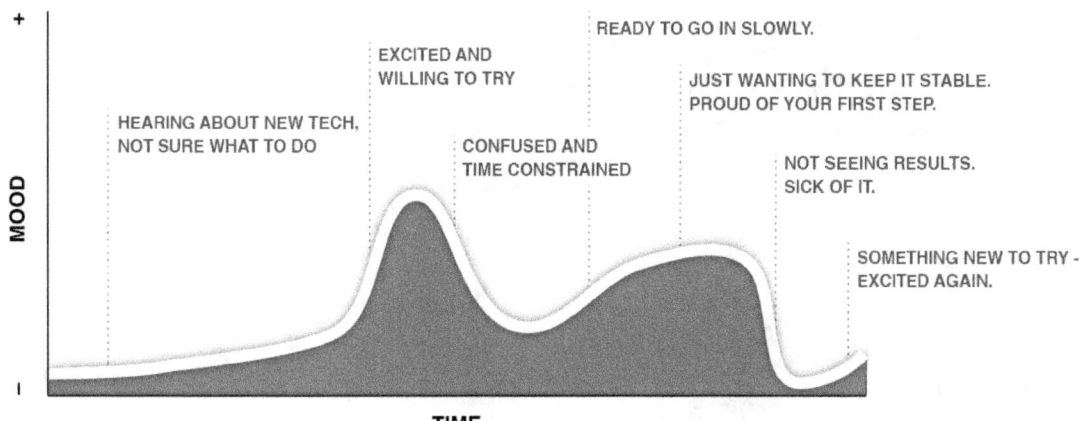

Exhibit 4 – Emotional cycles of technology adoption

As you can see from the diagram above, everyone goes through a series of emotions, ranging from excitement or intrigue all the way to confusion and frustration. It is cyclical, meaning that the vast majority of us go through ups and downs before we are fully acclimated to the new technology. The worst part is that we may go through this cycle several times over before a project is finished.

If you can see yourself at some point on this chart, then you probably have wanted some new technology but emotional and monetary issues could have made the decision around this new technology more difficult than it needs to be.

OK, on with the questions.

Question 1
What do you sell?

Every business sells something. It is the only way you can earn money and call it a business. The answer to this question should fit on a gum wrapper. Please, please do not write your mission statement or your unique selling proposition here! Keep it simple and just write down what your core product or service is.

Exhibit 5. Gum wrapper description of what you sell.

Examples of what to write on your gum wrapper:

I sell sandwiches.
I sell beauty products.
I teach piano.
I clean houses.
I paint homes.

What you write on the gum wrapper is not for an investor. It is essentially the way you would tell a two-year-old about your business. It is the simplest form, without any fancy adjectives or buzzwords. This is the core of what you do; keep it simple.

An example of what not to write is something like this "I sell up market plus size organic fair trade women's business attire in the Austin area." This just boils down to "I sell clothes."

Another example might be "I sell strategic marketing services to a wide variety of verticals on a performance basis, design and build websites, and blog." These are all things that you do, but which one drives the majority of your revenue and which one are you known for? The one your customer remembers should be your focus for this exercise.

If you can't fit your description on a gum wrapper, then you may not be sure what you truly sell. Ask friends for help with how they would describe your business in three to four words. Remember eliminate all the adjectives!

Question 2
Who are your customers?

This can actually be a complicated question, since many products or services appeal to a very large group of people. For instance, if you sell deli sandwiches, I am sure you have customers from age five all the way up to one hundred.

However, the main things to focus on here are the common attributes within your customer groups.

In reality, if you want to refine this question, it might make sense to ask it from a few different perspectives.

Ask yourself, do my customers do business with me because of my website or other online technologies? In other words, does your website currently generate any revenue for you? If so, let's write down what type of revenue it creates and how much it generates for you.

Example:
My website helps me _____ to my customers, which helps my business by
_____.

When looking at your core customer groups, it is important to think about the customer's lifestyle. If you don't want to assume, just ask them.

Question 3
Where is your business in terms of revenue or growth, and what are your expectations?

Take a step back for a moment. Look at where your business started and what it has become today. Has it grown in recent years, shrunk, or stayed somewhat flat? Knowing exactly what direction your company is moving is a great way to figure out if past investments are paying off.

Circle the graph that most closely resembles your business over the past year.

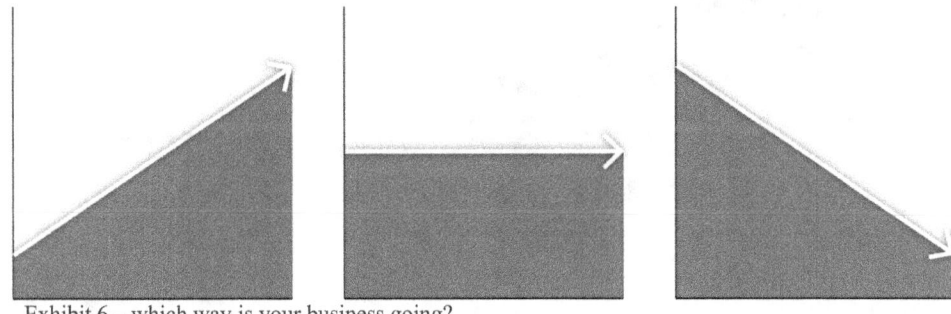

Exhibit 6 – which way is your business going?

More often than not, I hear from small business owners that they set up a website or another technology and nothing happened. It is always important to establish a current baseline to measure the success of a new project.

For example, let's say you want to implement some new technology for your corner deli. You realize sales have been flat for the past two years or so. You have experimented with new menu items, new décor, and even different pricing strategies. Nothing moved sales.

However, sometimes finding out what is affecting your business is about asking your customers, "What other restaurants do you guys go to around here?" and, most importantly, "Why?"

I have seen older delis around for decades that didn't notice that twenty other restaurants opened up within a two-mile radius in the past three years. Customers had more choice and took advantage of it. Remember, customers usually have a limited supply of time and money. As more competitive businesses vie for their dollars your share of the pie may potentially shrink.

Once you know where your company is from a growth perspective, we need to figure out where you want to go.

Do you want to grow sales with this new technology? Do you want to lure back former customers? Do you just want to take care of a request that many customers have been making?

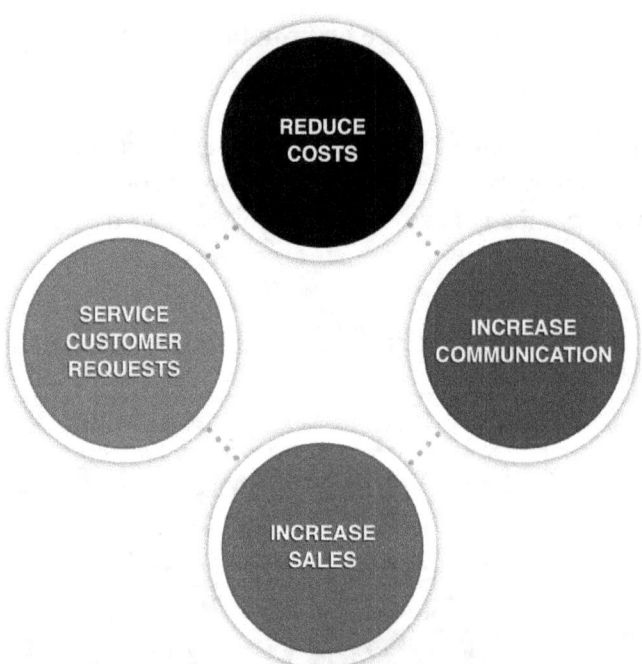

Exhibit 7. Macro-goals of a tech project.

Setting this goal or objective early on in the process is crucial to help simplify your decisions later on. Remember to attack only *one problem* at a time with technology, otherwise you can design things with hundreds of features that never go live or never get released.

For small businesses, the comparison might be adding a few products to your shelves at a time. You wouldn't change up your entire inventory overnight. That would be too expensive and too risky. Look at technology in the same way—dip your toes in first.

Here is an example evaluation of a current situation and an objective.

Current situation: My website is ten years old and doesn't reflect many of the things I have done in the past ten years.

Objective: Add more up-to-date content to the site.

Some people may immediately jump to the conclusion that you need to do a whole site redesign. But the short-term and cheapest problem to solve is just getting more updated content on the site.

Will a redesign be helpful? Probably yes, but it will take more time and money.

Make sure to tie that objective back to a goal. If you are adding more content to the site, what is your rationale for doing this? Will it provide customers with basic information they ask you on the phone? Then think, *Adding more content can potentially reduce my incoming phone calls and save me money.* The objective and the goal are slightly different but heavily intertwined.   To put it another way, the objective is the vision of where you want to be, and the goal is merely one step in the direction of your vision. Each vision must be broken down into multiple steps to be accomplished.

A major issue with this question is that most small business owners have expectations that they didn't set. Sometimes business owners get nervous that they are not moving fast enough. This might be an issue of a competitive business appearing to move faster. Very rarely will you have true insight into how the other business is doing. What this usually alludes to is that our mental picture of how our business should look doesn't align with our current resources.

The unfortunate outcome associated with this behavior is that we always feel like we are losing. This is not a good experience, and after a prolonged period of feeling like a loser, we often give up.

A way to end this vicious cycle is to be realistic about your resources and come up with a realistic image of where you want to be in the coming weeks.

The age-old goal is to make a million dollars. For many people, that may very well be possible, but this goal is often not attainable by many small businesses. Would you be happy with making $1,000 a week and potentially growing that to $1,500 a week over time? That would be a 50 percent gain and show that you are making the right decisions for your business. Now try to imagine all the steps needed to get from $1,500 to $1 million. Immediately, the path becomes less clear.

In other words, make your goals and visions your own. Don't worry about what the other person is doing. You own the playing field, so why not rig the game so you are always winning?

Just to reiterate, we are trying to figure out what your expectations are in terms of growth for your business.

Question 4
What does your brand stand for, or how are you known?

With small businesses, some know exactly what their brand stands for and some think they know exactly what their brand represents.

This not a mission or vision statement like you would put in a business plan. It is another gum-wrapper exercise.

Here are some ideas to get your mind going:

Are you known for honesty?
Are you known for a clean store?
Are you known for a great smile and being friendly?
Are you known for the latest products?
Are you known for being on time?

Exhibit 8. What your business is known for.

The list goes on, but pick one that your customers commonly say and try to build around it for now. This is not something set in stone but what you are known for right now. This is something you should capitalize on with any technology that you invest in.

Summary

Start the technology evaluation process by simply asking yourself where you are today and where you want to be in the near future. Keep it simple, and keep it honest. Keep in mind the most important facets here:

- What is your core offering?
- Who are your customers?
- Are you able to measure your current business or do you have a goal?
- What is your brand known for?

Use the chart below to help you gather your thoughts.

I sell_____.

My customers are_____.

I want my business to _____ over the next 6 months.

My brand is known for _____.

Chapter 2 - How Do You Measure Your Business?

The trouble with measurement is its seeming simplicity.
—Unknown

Measuring your business is probably one of the most misunderstood things these days.

People are bombarded with old and new metrics for measuring things in their business.

Usually the most basic measurements revolve around revenue and costs.

- How much money did you make today?
- How much did your sales cost you today?

Some of the new schools of thought say that you should measure the number of "shares" you get on Facebook posts and how many "retweets" you get on Twitter. If you don't know what a share or a retweet is, don't worry.

The point is, there are hundreds of metrics that you could measure your business by. It is hard to say which metrics are better than others, but there are some more universal metrics out there. This means that not only does everyone understand them, but you can also easily work with them.

Some universal metrics are the following:

- Revenue per day/month. How much you bring in per day and for the month. Pretty easy, right?
- Total costs per month. This includes all your fixed overhead, like rent and staff. It also includes variable overhead, like cost of goods, electricity, Internet, cell phone, etc.
- Number of sales per month. This is how many unique people bought something from you this month. This also helps you figure out if you are growing your customer base or revenue base on a per month basis.

Examples of specialty metrics include:

- Unique website visitors per month. This is used in online advertising quite often. It usually relates to how much you can charge advertisers.
- Revenue per square foot. A lot of retailers look at this figure to find out how much money they are making per day or month per square foot of their retail space. This is why you sometimes see some stores which are packed wall to wall with products and some stores which have just a few items which are very expensive.

- Machine hours. Usually a measure of how long a particular machine has been used. It usually determines a depreciation value or time left before a costly repair.

What is the key to business metrics? Which one should you choose?

Business metrics are a data junkie's dream. A person can sit there, dissect a lot of things about each business, and then finally end up in "paralysis by analysis."

The downside to knowing too much, in terms of metrics, is that you can spend a lot of time per day either gathering the metrics or just looking at them. More often than not, I see business owners get interested in and addicted to metrics, then realize that business is not improving.

Why?

Simple, because they are looking at metrics and not the customers.

Choosing actionable metrics is a process. The good thing is that it doesn't take all that long to do.

Step 1
We need to gather a list of things you want to measure in your business. This is a list of wants. Consider it a wish list. Assume you have unlimited time and money to monitor these metrics.

Put your wish list of metrics here:

Metric	Why I want it?
_____	_____
_____	_____
_____	_____
_____	_____
_____	_____
_____	_____

Step 2
Assign roles. Who in your organization is going to look at the metrics? What is his or her title? Will he or she have the power to effect change?

Sometimes the role and the title will be the same thing, but sometimes we have frivolous titles like "account management" that might entail a much larger role or greater responsibilities.

In the chart below, the power to execute is referring to the person's ability to make a decision and create the change. In some companies people like to make decisions to only realize that no one will actually help them implement or enforce the change.

Role	Title	Power to Execute
		Yes No
Role	Title	Power to Execute
		Yes No
Role	Title	Power to Execute
		Yes No
Role	Title	Power to Execute
		Yes No

Step 3

Create a time budget. Just like you monitor your spending for your store, you should limit how much time you will devote to measuring your business. If you have no idea where to start with this, I would suggest a downward scale. There is a learning curve involved in this, so budget one to two hours in the first few days and then back down to ten to fifteen minutes per day when you get the hang of it. If it is taking you more than fifteen minutes a day to know what is going on with your business, you are looking at too many metrics.

Step 4

Review your business goals. Is your personal job to increase sales this month or to increase the profit or cut costs? Is it to create more smiles?

Your short-term goal can be anything. But it is important to have some sort of general objective or goal, which helps you focus everything you are spending time on.

Step 5

Now the fun part!

Time to start slashing your list of wants down. You will have two ways of cutting down this list. I suggest you do them in order to help keep things clear.

To start shortening the list of desired metrics, you want to start by asking yourself which ones have nothing to do with your short-term goal/objective. This should really eliminate 80 percent of your desired metrics.

Don't fool yourself by saying that X metric is tied to your goal through a convoluted path. You must be able to see a direct path between your metric and goal!

Remember the goal here is to cut away stuff, not save it for later.

Step 5 is to really look at your short list and see which of these metrics is actionable. When I say actionable, I mean which ones can you really act on and make a change with daily?

If your metric gives you data you can act upon but it might take you three months to change a process, it is probably not something you want to measure daily. I would save that metric for a monthly review meeting.

Within your short list, I would guess that only one or two metrics relate to your core goal, and maybe only one can be acted upon every day.

Here is a quick example for a deli:

Goal: Increase sales per day of a new bottled ice tea.

Potential metrics:

- Number of bottles in the fridge.
- Cost per bottle.
- Time on shelf.
- Number of drinks sold per day/per month.
- Drinks sold at lunch.
- Fountain drinks versus bottled drinks sold.
- Number of sandwiches sold.
- Average revenue per customer.
- Number of male/female customers per day.
- Number of adults versus kid customers per day.
- Number of ice tea bottles sold per day.

As you can see, the list can keep going.

Short list of potential metrics:

- Fountain drinks versus bottled drinks sold.
- Number of ice tea bottles sold per day.

The reason I chose these two metrics is because they are easy to measure and they give me information directly about my goal of selling more ice tea bottles per day. To measure them, all I need is to keep a tally with a piece of paper and a pencil.

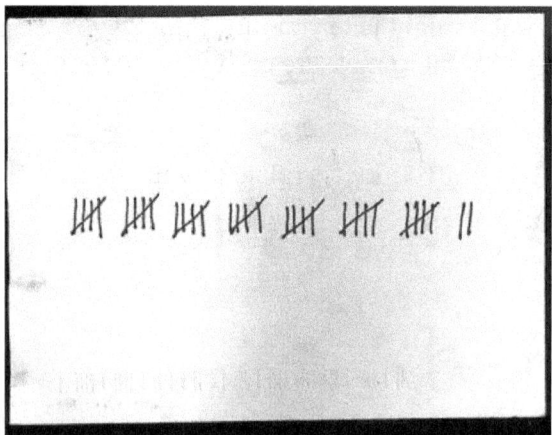

Exhibit 9. Tally it up!

Back to the goal, the deli needs to sell more bottles of ice tea per day.

Now I am actively measuring the bottles per day, and usually it makes sense to measure them by hour.

This helps you see a trend during the day and whether you're above or below pace for your goal.

For instance, by 11:00 a.m., you have sold ten bottles on day one.
On day two, by 11:00 a.m., you have sold fifteen bottles.

There is progress, but did you change anything? Was it warmer that day? Were you out of other bottled drinks? Did you change the price? Did you tell your customers about the new ice tea?

Any strategy you take toward meeting your goal is now measurable via your tally on paper. One possible way you can increase sales of this new bottled drink is to tell your cashier to offer each customer your "new ice cold bottled drink for only a dollar more." Usually the mere suggestion of something new is enough to push a customer to try it once and therefore increase sales. Another strategy might be to update your signage to include that you are now carrying this new bottled drink. Customers need to know about your new offerings, and it will be up to you as a business owner to test out offerings to see what creates the largest increase in sales. The good news is that you are now creating actionable metrics. Congratulations!

Remember, if you can't measure it, you can't improve it. So stop *worrying about it!*

Before letting you off into the wild with this, I wanted to let you know that it is somewhat dangerous to choose a vague goal or a goal that takes too much time to measure. The danger is that you will get distracted over time or you wont be able to act on your metric. Any metric that you need weeks or months to measure may not be a good starting point. I strongly suggest as you test these methodologies that you focus on testing things with time frames of less than one day. Once again, keep it simple and keep it actionable!

Summary

Measuring your business is an important task. First, understand the goal and then define the metric that can easily be collected and acted upon. Keep it simple and short-term. A long-term goal is a want. A short-term goal is how you are going to get there.

Chapter 3 - The Dramatic Pause

Courage is the discovery that you may not win, and trying when you know you can lose. —Tom Krause

Some people might think what I am about to say is nuts.

Recall the first two chapters. We evaluated where your business currently stands and tried to come up with a metric and goal.

It's OK if you are struggling to find a connection between a technology and your business, or you are not able to measure what technology does for you. It might be a good time to put this book down and actually get back to your customers, work on your core product or service. Stop worrying about technology.

In other words, it is OK to stop reading this book.

The one note of caution here is that I want you to mark your calendar to come back to this book in a month to see if anything has changed. If you see that something has dramatically changed, and a connection from technology to your business has appeared, then start reading again!

The rest of this book focuses on defining your tech project, picking a team, and monitoring your results. It is written in layperson's terms and meant to provide you with advice that will save you time and money.

Summary
Decide if this is the *right time* in your business to read this book. If not, simply make a reminder to read it in the future. It will help you eventually.

So what will it be—read or reminder?

Chapter 4 - What Is Your Marketing History?

A careful inventory of all your past experiences may disclose the startling fact that everything has happened for the best.
—Unknown

Sometimes when we are building a plan for the future, we need to look at what the business has done in the past. Most small businesses are bombarded with various types of marketing mechanisms, ranging from a website to a coupon mailer to a phone book listing.

Many times, the prices are too good to pass up, so we try out an offer and hope for the best. Internally, our expectations are quite high, but all we are thinking about is more customers. That's a very vague goal, and the timeline associated with it is even more vague. Would you consider a coupon mailer a success if ten people showed up with the coupon over six months?

Meeting with small business owners, it is easy to see that they are not sure how to convey their brand or product in a very small amount of space. Most online ads have to be less than a hundred characters—not words, but characters. That is tiny!

Sample search ad c. 2012.

2013 Ford Mustang
www.ford.com/Mustang
Amazing, Powerful, Legendary.
Mustang Never Disappoints!

Exhibit 10. Google AdWords ad circa June 2012.

For direct mail, most people would say if your headline is longer than five words, your ad is not read at all.

Think for a minute, how can you summarize your business in less than five words? (Hint: refer back to your gum wrapper!)

To get a better understanding of what you have already tried, let's go down this checklist:

What types of media have you used in the past?

Traditional Offline Media:
Direct mail
Coupons
TV
Radio
Billboards

Newspaper
Phone calls
Frequent buyer cards
Giveaways
Seminars
Magazines
PR

Online:
Banners
E-mails
Social display ads
Search ads
Reviews
Online PR
Online coupon codes
Affiliate marketing
Website

Look at the Exhibit 15 below. It highlights the building blocks of a brand. It is a simplistic view of things, but it shows how everything else builds upon the foundational elements. Each additional thing must draw its concept from the foundational elements. The blocks that you add on the top must fit, almost like Lego® blocks, to ensure a consistent structure. In many regards, the structure is very similar to a Lego® block tower, since you choose when to add to a particular section and how much to add. Keep this in mind as you continue to build your brand image. If something doesn't fit or draw consistently from the foundation of your business, it is OK to pass it up and move on.

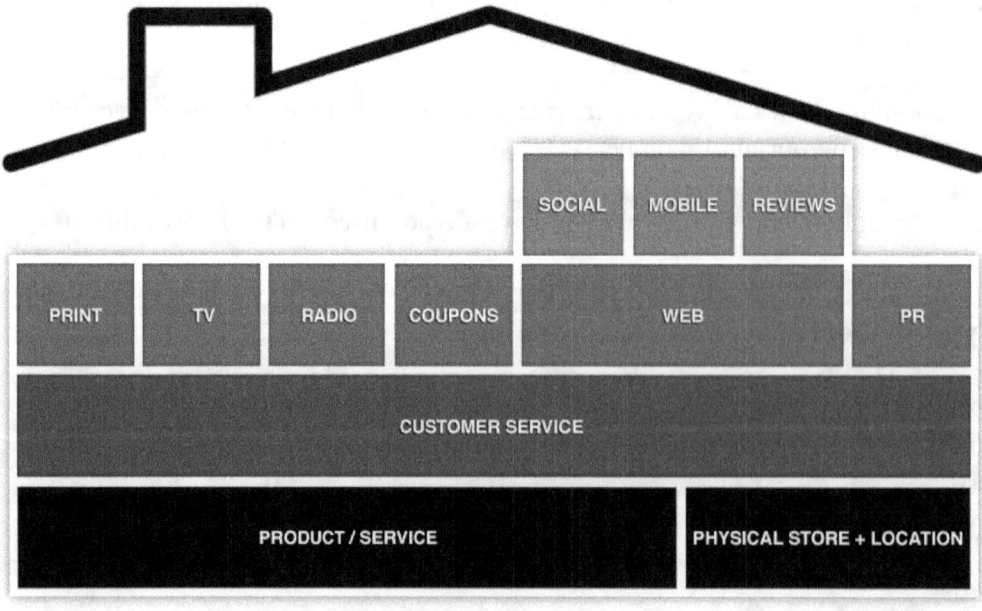

Exhibit 11. Branding blocks—just like building a house!

In Exhibit 11, it is important to note that the product/service along with customer service are at the base of the house. These elements really provide the foundation of what you are known for and help you align any marketing efforts in the future. Each marketing dollar you spend must align with or build upon your foundation.

At the moment, I put social and mobile on top of web since I see them as subcomponents. The web will continue to expand but it is important to see how the web relates to the rest of your media strategy which includes print, tv, radio, coupons and PR. The web will always be just one facet or component of your marketing, if you depend on it too much, you may not be getting full exposure.

Now we have an idea of what you have done in the past with your marketing, lets hop into the benefits and costs.

How much did you spend?

When looking at your spending, you want to consider how much you were actually billed, the discounts you gave away, and any creative costs. This will give you a total cost for each advertisement.

Example costs of an advertisement:

Cost to purchase quarter-page newspaper ad	$2000
Graphic design	$500
Discount—20 percent off, which equaled	$5,000
Total advertising costs	$7,500
Total new revenue	$25,000
Revenue minus advertising costs(Profit)	$17,500

Your spending should also be normalized so you can really compare apples to apples later on. For instance, if you spent $200 on one thousand postcards, your cost per person was twenty cents.

If you spent $100 on five thousand e-mails, your cost per person would be only two cents.

How long ago was it?
Did your last ad go out two days or twelve months ago?

What was the message?

What were you promoting in your last advertisement? Was it introducing your business, saying something like "Grand opening!" or was it a seasonal promotion, like for a Mother's Day sale?

What was the call to action?
One of the most important things you can do in any advertisement is make sure you have a call to action. A call to action is simply what you want the consumer to do after reading your advertisement.

Example calls to action are buy a sandwich on Tuesday and get a free drink. A bad call to action would be "come on in." It doesn't really tell the consumer to buy something, which may make your advertisement less effective.

What was your metric?
How did you measure the outcome of the advertisement? Did you count how many people redeemed a coupon? Did you look at sales before and after the advertisement? Did you ask customers if they had seen the advertisement?

More importantly, did you have a goal for your metric? Did you want to achieve a 5 percent sales increase as your goal, or was your promotion without a goal? Another metric might be, did you make your money back on the advertisement?

Did you achieve that metric?
It's pretty simple to assess if you actually met your metric. If you didn't achieve your metric, do you have any insight into why it didn't work? Did you ask your customers why they didn't see or use the advertisement? Did another company have a similar or better promotion at the same time?

Did you get any customer feedback on it?
Did you mail out the advertisement or launch it online? Did it even reach your customers? A simple way to test for this is to ask your customers "Did you see X?" Ask a wide group of people before making a conclusion.

Did you try it again or renew it?
Amazingly, a lot of business owners keep advertising even without knowing how the last advertisement worked. Sometimes this is a good strategy, since you just flood the market with your brand name and tend to get a large share of mind. Sometimes it's a massive waste of money. It is OK to be honest here. You are only reporting to yourself.

Once you get a better idea of what you have done in the past, you will have an idea of what you can potentially build upon.

If the majority of your advertising has been coupon-oriented, people may now associate your brand with heavy discounts. I call this the Bed Bath & Beyond pricing model. That company sends out 20 percent coupons all the time, so people wait until the coupon comes out to shop there.

Exhibit 12. Bed Bath & Beyond 20 percent-off coupon mailer.

If your branding has been mainly online-based, you may be missing a large audience that doesn't go online often or doesn't visit the specific website where you advertised.

The key to this exercise is understanding if your previous work has provided any return at all and how it portrayed your brand.

Summary
Taking a look at the past can give you several clues about what works for your business and what you can improve upon. Reflection is a powerful tool. Use it!

If you start to see a pattern of experimenting with a lot of new technologies but nothing was really working out, I want you to take a step back. I want you as a business owner to consider if it makes sense to spend more and more money on new technology if you don't have time to foster or monitor them. What happens if you turn that energy and money towards improving your core product or service? Would that be something you enjoy more?

Chapter 5 - Phone Book Technologies

It will take a long time for old technology to disappear.
—Steve Snider

I dare you to do a search on Amazon for books about social media. Hundreds of results! Holy crap, which book is the right book? Should I just go with the one with the most reviews?

Stop!

Why the hell are you looking at social media? You may know what social media is, and it might fit really well with your business. But how are your phone book technologies doing?

Phone books? Seriously?

Yes.

I am not asking you to invest in a phone book advertisement, but I am asking you to check that your most basic advertising methods have been fully exploited and updated before you move into the online space. As more and more people move their advertising dollars online, you will see traditional media become a bit cheaper and still retain its effectiveness.

Why? Because online media is almost never a solitary brand-building machine. Brands are developed from multiple points or facets. The facets work together to provide a brand image for the consumer.

Let's say that you only focus on coupon mailers for your business. Perhaps your consumers now think you are a small local retailer. What happens when you add TV to the mix? All of a sudden, you seem a bit more legitimate, a bit larger, a bit more honest, a bit more "real."

What happens when you mix in radio advertising? Newspaper advertising? More legitimacy.

Lastly, you decide to experiment with online ads. Consumers are now more willing to click the ad because they know you are a real company and are somewhat familiar with your brand through all the other advertising.

When I talk about phone book technologies, I am mainly referring to things that bolster your image and are universally understood.

One of my personal favorites of the old-school technologies is face-to-face interaction. Channeling a bit of Dale Carnegie, the smile is an infectious little tool we all can use. It is amazingly effective, and is used in every culture. Best of all, it is free.

Focusing on the brief moments when you are able to meet your customer face-to-face, give them one of those free smiles.

Exhibit 13. Brand-influence facets.

As you can see from Exhibit 13 above, your customer is exposed to your brand through many different avenues. Each time the consumer is exposed or touched by your brand it helps achieve two main brand builders. It helps create legitimacy or trust with the consumer and it helps increase share of mind.

Legitimacy and trust are incredibly important these days since it eventually relates back to quality perception. Your brand is not your product itself but how your product works. In our deli example, your product is a sandwich, but the consistency of freshness and top quality ingredients helps define your brand. If you ever serve a sandwich that is not fresh or uses cut rate ingredients, you risk destroying the trust you have with your customer and losing a loyal return customer.

When discussing the share of mind, it is important to remember that your customers have several choices during the course of a day. When they are hungry, you want them to think of your sandwich place first and ultimately buy from you. Lets say there are three other delis within a 5-mile radius that your customers could choose from. Out of the three delis, you are the only one who decides to advertise on TV, radio, online and in the newspaper. Your two other competitors don't do any advertising. From the consumer point of view, they see and hear about you much more during each day and the likelihood of them remembering you first is greater. Through your multi-faceted marketing approach, you have increased your share of mind.

As a business owner, you might think, if my competitor is not advertising at all, do I need to be so aggressive and buy all that advertising? Part of your advertising is to ensure you are attracting new customers, part of it is making sure your existing customers keep coming back and the last part is devoted to making sure your competitors don't steal your customers. It is a bit of an offensive strategy, occupying your consumers mind so they don't even consider the alternative. The ultimate goal is to get to 100% share of mind with your consumer. Similar to what Coca Cola has done with many people. When they are asked if they would like a drink, many people simply answer "yes, a Coke please." They don't even think about the other choices, it has become their default answer when they think they are thirsty.

If you look at Exhibit 13 again, you will notice that customer reviews is a facet of influence. In today's online world, customer reviews are becoming more and more important in terms of driving a consumer's brand perception. As a deli owner, you may offer an amazing sandwich, but for some reason your online reviews have turned negative. I have seen in certain markets that competitors will actually go into sites like Yelp and Google and write negative reviews to sabotage your business. This can be problematic to your business and should be addressed immediately.

As a brand owner and creator, you must take proactive and reactive steps to ensure your brand image is consistent. This can be hard to do when your brand is in so many places at once.

The information below will discuss how your brand image is developed in a person's mind. Brand influence and how a consumer interacts with you these days is incredibly multifaceted.

What Google and Bing—the two largest search engines—do every day is try to determine the most relevant website for any particular search term. To do this, they are essentially looking at the legitimacy of your brand, trying to figure out how and whom you influence. They are also looking at the quality of your website in terms of originality. Without going into too much detail, they attempt to establish your sphere of influence by using several online factors. These online factors are mere reflections of your real-world product or service. For example, if you have a great product, your customers will talk about it online. These conversations go into Google's system and start to create a picture of how the search engine should view you and where it should rank you.

Are there ways of rigging the results? Yes. But, long-term, the best way to be consistently considered the best or more relevant is to focus on quality first. Quality in your product, quality in your brand, quality in your customer service, and each of the above facets in exhibit 13.

What I want to talk about here is how you can really create a solid foundation for your brand by focusing on some foundational elements first.

Imagine this scenario. You're in Detroit, Michigan, in the dead of winter. The thermometer reads five degrees, and even though it's only noon, the sky is gray and dreary. Looking to thaw out, you walk into a coffee shop and are greeted by the counter person with a smile so warm, you almost forget why you stepped into the establishment in the first place. All it took was a smile to change your attitude. You saddle up to the counter and enjoy the conversation…and a hot cup of coffee.

In addition to smiles, here are some universal technologies that I think every small business needs to invest in to bolster its online brand.

- Press releases - The world of PR is largely a mystery to most small businesses. Most of the time, people think they don't have something that special to talk about, so they are worried about not being relevant.

The fact is that PR can be achieved in many ways. It can be in the form of an interview with your local newspaper, or it can be showing up at a charity event in your town. As long as people recognize you and associate you with your business, you are performing a form of PR. Local papers and magazines are hungry for content. They will usually be excited to interview you about your new sandwich or how the new neighborhood is affecting your business. Any PR is good PR. Most of the time if you focus on creating a quality product and you are able to educate your consumer about the differences that make your product amazing, you can get good PR coverage.

The objectives of PR are to build the messages you want your consumers to hear, and then to get your name out there by establishing yourself as an expert within your industry.

For example, if you run a summer camp, your core customers are parents with kids between seven and seventeen years old. Leading up to the summer, you talk to your local paper about how to choose the best summer camp for your seven year old. While discussing the top five ways to pick a summer camp, you explain your camp's unique qualities. As a secondary benefit, you might talk about the things parents do while the kids are at camp, such as date nights and reading the Sunday paper.

The end result is that you've established yourself as a knowledgeable and credible source about summer camps, but you have also provided readers of the article the benefits of choosing your camp.

• Print, magazines or newspapers - Print advertising is going through some massive changes these days. Print media readership is down, and the circulation numbers are dropping fast. Why recommend it? Because it is still seen as a discovery tool. Often, I pick up a magazine at the bookstore, browse through it, and don't buy it. But I might take note of an ad or interesting product that I had never seen before. I still learn a great deal through newspapers, but I don't enjoy paying for the information. Fifteen years ago, the $1.00 charge was nominal and just expected. The medium still has value, but it is getting harder and harder for me to actually purchase the paper since we can get the information free online.

There is a sphere that most people live in online, visiting the same sites, talking to the same friends, and seeing a small subset of advertisements. Similarly, magazines and newspapers usually cover things that are relevant to you at a category level, such as technology. A technology magazine addresses issues about technology companies, goods, and services. It focuses on informing the consumer about new or noteworthy products or services. We put a bit of trust into a magazine by assuming it's curating the information to fit within the magazine.

In other words, print publications help you expand your sphere of information through advertisements, PR pieces, and original writing. If I saw a product mentioned in a magazine and then saw an advertisement for it online, I would once again think it more legitimate than if I just saw it online. A secondary source of information (the magazine) verified that the product was legitimate, and I put some trust in the magazine.

One must also consider the original model of journalism that was based not on speed but on research, and vetting of a particular topic. Magazines had to make sure what they were printing was true otherwise they could damage the trust with the reader. Today's blogs do not adhere to the same standards since their core focus is on being the first to break a story, even if it is not true or fully correct. As the US's definition of journalism evolves, it becomes important to understand what your customers truly trust and what they are legitimately influenced by. This helps you better understand where to allocate marketing dollars for maximum impact.

• Television - TV is one of the most amazing forms of media available today. The content is incredibly rich, it has structure, everyone knows what a TV does, and almost everyone in the USA has a TV. Being on TV gives you instant credibility and allows you to convey your product or service with video, one of the richest forms of content. A rich piece of content involves motion, sound, multiple ways to contact the company, and usually has more impact than a black and white newspaper ad for example. You can choose to do a short commercial or a longer infomercial.

Most people are scared of TV since they think it costs a ton and they have no idea where to start with the production of a TV commercial. Is TV really expensive? Yes and no. You can easily hire an expensive ad agency, produce an amazing thirty-second commercial, and then buy expensive airtime on a prime time show. All in all, you can easily spend millions of dollars for thirty seconds.

In the past twenty years, hundreds of new channels have appeared, and their biggest problem is that they can't sell all of the ad space. This is your biggest opportunity. Local TV stations often look for local businesses to advertise with them. They assist you in producing your commercial, or they readily recommend local videographers. My suggestion here is to start local. Work with local universities to find students studying film who will make your commercial for next to nothing. Members of local communities always help each other.

As the TV market continues to evolve, there are many more choices for you as an advertiser. Google now offers you the ability to buy TV advertising through their platform. To find out more about this, please check out http://www.google.com/ads/tv/.

• Radio - Radio is another technology that many consider obsolete. However, you are probably asking people who are on the cutting edge of things. Every car in the US has a radio, and people spend a lot of time in their cars. Radio, especially local radio, is a great way of talking about current promotions. Live radio is a flexible medium. Once again, the goal is not to come up with an amazing commercial for radio but to focus on being mentioned, being timely, and being local. All you are looking for is a person to remember your company's name. If that person actually comes in and buys something, great, but the short-term goal is to get into the customer's head and become a legitimate brand.

• A notepad - How is a notepad relevant technology? The core tenet of this book is that your customer is your best source of knowledge and feedback. If you don't take a moment to write down that valuable feedback, you are allowing it to just disappear.

Summary:
Old School technologies should not be discounted. They help build and reinforce your brand online. Usually local is better and cheaper in some cases. Knowing your customer is a key component to designing any brand.

Chapter 6 - What Are Your Current Technical Assets?

Being properly prepared is one of the biggest assets in business and in athletic competition. – Keeth Smart

When deciding if you need to invest in technology, you should look at many factors. One place to start is an inventory of what technical assets you hold currently.

Technical assets are really broken up into two main categories: elements that support your brand and elements that grow your brand.

For example, take the hierarchy of different technologies below.

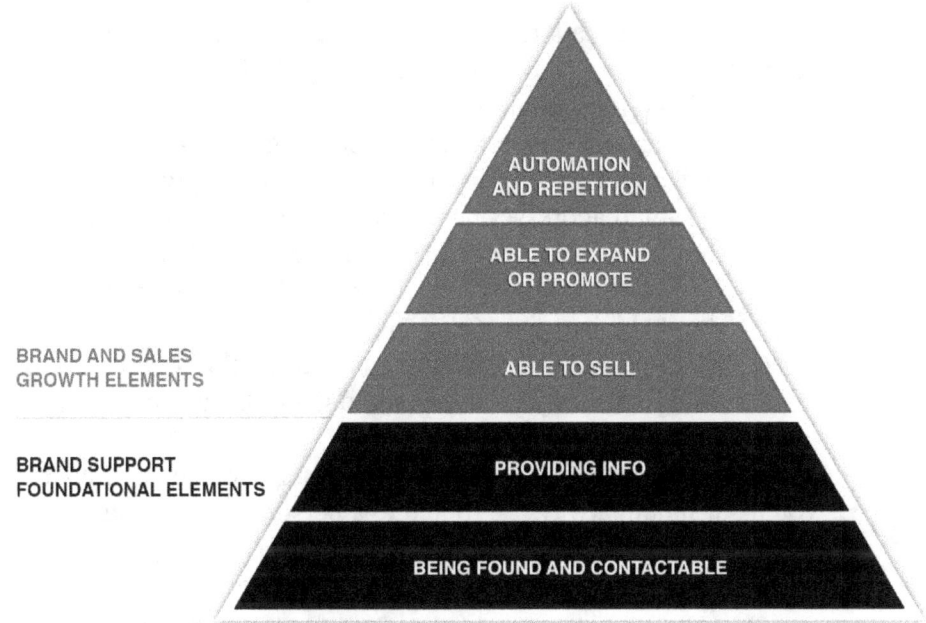

Exhibit 14. Old School Simple's technology hierarchy.

The bottom two categories are focused on supporting your brand through supplying the customer basic information, such as where you are located, how to contact you, and what you might be selling. At the very least, your technology should be providing this.

Once you move up to the yellow section, you start to offer your customers more than their needs and focus on building sales and growing the brand. The technology at this level should help you sell more and find new customers. The ultimate point on the hierarchy is a technology that allows you to achieve all of the levels below in an easily repeatable or automated way. With today's technology, this is the Holy Grail and is often not executed well.

Staying focused on the lower levels is less experimental and usually provides a better consumer experience. As you move up the hierarchy, risk increases and potential returns may actually decrease if execution is not perfect. As you move up the pyramid, the risk increases and the need for quicker feedback loops becomes more important.

Given that the upper levels are always in flux and somewhat risky, I have put together a list of technologies that focus on the primary or essential levels. This includes things as basic as the sign on your door, technology items your customers expect.

The Essentials List

- Communication technology - In general, people need to get in contact with you for a variety of reasons. These core technologies have been around for quite some time, and it can be said that they are now standards.
    - E-mail - When I talk to small businesses, most have an e-mail address of some sort. Here are a few issues I often see:
        —No one is monitoring the e-mail address. This is just a bad customer experience. If you are going to list this e-mail address publicly, check it often and reply!
        —E-mail addresses not on your company domain. You should always have an e-mail address that is the same as your brand. If your deli is called Joe's Deli, your e-mail should be joe@joesdeli.com, not JJ9128yasdh@yahoo.com. Not making this simple change makes your company look outdated and unprofessional.
    - Phone - Every small business has a phone. The phone number you have should always be routed to a person who is going to answer. If, for some reason, setting up call forwarding is not possible, make sure your phone calls are always answered by a custom recording that states your hours of operation, your website URL, and your physical location. Those pieces of information will address most people's needs.

- Location technology.
    - Map - One of the most common things people want to know about your business is its location. There are a few things you can do to make sure a person can find your business. On your website, make the address easy to find by including directions from common locations or a map.
        —You can use a hand-drawn map or one from a mapping website that allows you to place its digital map on your site.
        —Google also offers what is called a Place Page. This is like a free phone book listing, but it has some important information attached to it. It includes your location, a few pictures, reviews, phone number, a link to your website,

and a map. You can get your free Google Place Page here: http://www.google.com/places/.

• Branded website - Ah, now we are at the part where everyone cringes. Your business needs a website. There is no way around this. But the good thing is that you don't have to be afraid of this. I am not only going to walk you through the process of setting up a website, but I am also going to tell you the most important foundational elements.

A house foundation is created in conjunction with how the final product should look. The foundational elements of a website must work in unison with your core business.

Exhibit 15 - House Foundation

A corporate website should be thought of like a front door to your business. Without a door, people have trouble purchasing things from you since they can't get in. Every good business door should have a few pieces of simple information:

—Name - This is your URL or domain. This must coordinate with the name of your business. Making it simple for your customers to remember is important.

— Basic information - Each website must contain your business contact information, hours, location, information about your brand or product, and information about you, the owner.

Deciding what information to include about your product or service can be daunting. In our deli example, it would probably be important to provide a menu. If you are struggling about what type of content your customers may want to see, simply ask them!

One key ideal about the architecture of your site is to keep it as simple as possible.

There is a ton of technology that is considered "optional." When I say it is optional, I mean not all of your customers will expect it, but some may find it very useful. When the vast majority of your customers expect something, you should no longer consider it optional and move it over to your priority list.

As of 2012, I personally consider social media technologies largely optional. For most small businesses, it is nice to have a presence on the platforms, but they are very time-consuming. I also don't see huge financial returns from these systems for small businesses. Lastly, not everyone expects your business to be on Facebook, Twitter, or Google+. It is a nice feature, but, in reality, I am still more comfortable doing business with the local deli face-to-face.

Summary

Taking a quick inventory of your technology assets is a good way to see if you have your bases covered. Are you spending money and time on things that don't provide a return? Are your systems updated?

These are easy-to-answer questions that usually highlight several short-term projects that can refocus your business. They can also highlight what you want compared to what your customers truly need. Make sure the wants and needs match up as much as possible.

Chapter 7 - The $199 Offer

There is nothing in the world that some man cannot make a little worse and sell a little cheaper and he who considers price only is that man's lawful prey.
—John Ruskin

During a recent interview with a small business, I realized that people are so daunted by technology they fall back on pricing as their main decision metric.

When you use pricing as your main criteria, you instantly become susceptible to offers like the $199 website. These deals are very common, coming from companies that offer business cards as their main product or checkbooks or yellow page listings or domains.

The reason why $199 websites exist is because a website, in general, is somewhat of a commodity at the start. It has a home page, Contact Us page, About Us page, and some basic info about your product or services. Since this information is so rudimentary, often it is put into a template of sorts. This template offers a bit of customization with some color choices and minor graphic options. But, for the most part, you are stuck in a somewhat rigid structure when you use one.

The template requires that you make some choices, the same choices you might have made with a regular web agency or web developer.

There are many benefits to the template websites available these days:
- The site gets done quickly. You can reasonably put up a site within four to six hours, including all of your writing. Some people can do it within one to two hours, but, realistically, it is a one-day project.
- It gets you into a framework and can give you a starting point.
- It allows you to quickly visualize how the site might work and look.
- It is cheap.

There are downsides to choosing a template website that you should be aware of too:
- You get what you pay for. The site will work, but it may not look professional.
- It may not accurately represent your brand.
- Customers don't usually see it as a high-quality product. It often looks like what it is—a template. This can make the company seem unprofessional.
- You may have to rebuild it in a few months. It is often seen as a stopgap solution.
- If it is a bad template, it may not appear correctly on all computers or devices.
- It may not include the newest social technologies. These templates are standalone sites that are not fully integrated with the major search

engines or social sites. This could really hurt your ability to be found on the Internet.

- If you want to add a shopping cart experience, it will require additional customization and time.
- The cost to customize a template is almost on par with building a custom site from scratch. I personally priced out a $199 template with customizations and it came out to nearly $1500 and would take 4 weeks to complete. To me there wasn't much of a cost savings by taking the template approach.

Overall, templates are not a bad option, but they are often shortsighted or temporary solutions.

I am not going to tell you to fully avoid them, but use them as a stepping-stone if you must. I think they are great tools to help small business owners start thinking about what information they want to present online. The templates almost resemble an "Mad Libs book" type process, where they give you 80 to 90 percent of the structure and you complete the rest.

If you do use a template as a tool to get some thoughts down and online quickly, please make sure you eventually take the time to invest in a longer-term, more professional solution. Your business is unique, and your brand image online should reflect that.

Summary

It is OK to test out a cheap website template, but don't think it will last long-term. Use it is a stepping-stone to a more customized project.

Chapter 8 - Let Technology News Come to You

What information consumes is rather obvious: it consumes the attention of its recipients. Hence a wealth of information creates a poverty of attention and a need to allocate that attention efficiently among the overabundance of information sources.
—Unknown

One topic that has been somewhat frustrating for me to write about is finding information on available technology.

Then it dawned on me. I don't have to look any further than the customers in front of me. But which ones might give me the best information?

I struggled to determine the most fruitful "information feeders."

Finding information feeders is a bit like farming; some fields will yield value for a long time, and some will go barren very quickly. Some people get stuck in a certain technology and stop listening for new stuff. This is usually directly correlated to age. As you get older, you realize you don't have as much time to be on the bleeding edge of technology, nor do you have the monetary resources to test all the new stuff.

Finding feeders is usually a multifaceted prospect. There are both business and personal technologies that you may want to know about. Where these technologies intersect is where you want to focus your questions.

Exhibit 16. Business and consumer tech combined is where the real value is.

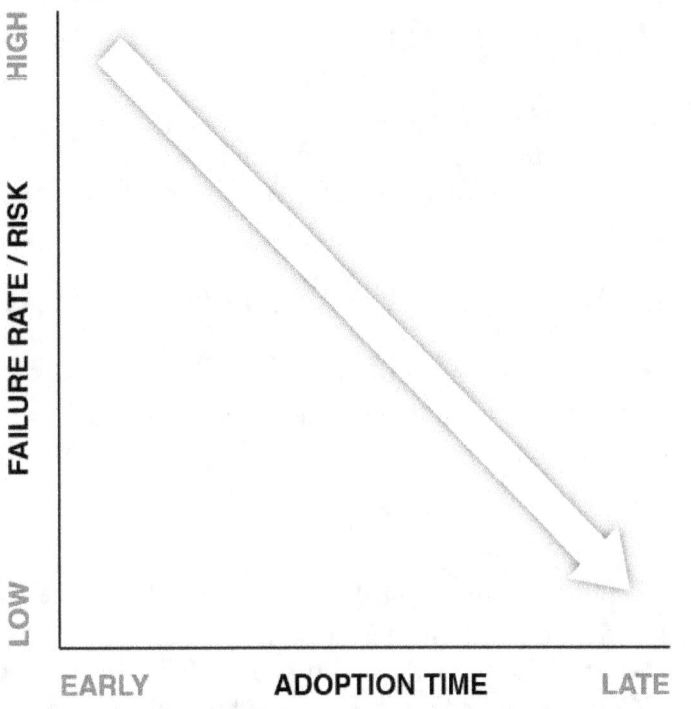

Exhibit 17. Being early or late—how much risk do you want?

First level feeders
Vocal consumers. Your most valuable information feeders are the customers in your shop. There are two ways of getting information from them that could be beneficial for you.

First, observation and questions:

- Observe whether they are using devices like a computer, phone, or tablet.
- Ask them if the device influences how they shop with you in any way.
- Observe whether they are using jargon that you are not familiar with—for example, "I am checking in here."
- Ask them what the jargon means and what they get out of it.
- Ask them if it would be helpful if your business was on that system.

Remember to use your notepad to write down answers from these conversations. Sometimes you may want to look at a few people deep into your line at your shop to see what they are doing. Usually, people occupy waiting time with other activities, especially if they are alone.

Exhibit 18. People often check their phones while waiting in line. Why not approach them?
http://www.thedatingtruth.com/wp-content/uploads/2011/04/people-texting.jpg

Second level feeders
Other businesses. If your business is next to other businesses, you probably have similar customers, to some extent.

Asking the other business owners and staff what they are doing technology-wise will help you create a more vivid picture of which technology you should pay attention to.

The greatest part is that you can always work these questions into daily conversations.

Use what you gained from the level one feeders and see if the other business owners can validate it.

For example, "I heard about this checking-in thing. Do you guys use that system at all? Does it help you drive any revenue?"

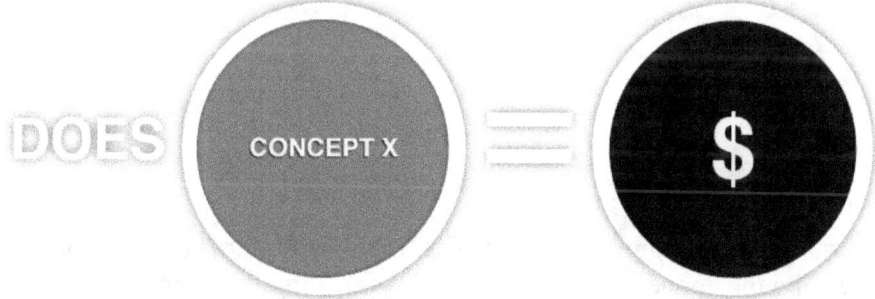

Exhibit 19. What is the connection?

More often than not, they have heard of the new system and may even be using it, but they are rarely driving new revenue with it.

This becomes a quick and cheap way to eliminate a lot of technologies that will waste your time.

Now, most people will say if no one tested new technology, the market as a whole would not move forward. This is true.

The catch here is that you should ask the same question multiple times to verify that the answer is still valid.

Opinions and adoption rates change. Knowing when to strike and test out a new technology can be a big cost-saver by itself.

For example, in 2006, the majority of small businesses probably did not even know what Facebook was. In 2012, the vast majority of businesses know what it is, but only handfuls are driving new or real revenue from it.

If you were a company entering Facebook in 2006, your risk of investing in the wrong place was very high, and the outcomes were very uncertain. In other words, your potential for failure or wasting time learning the wrong system was very high.

In 2012, the platform is large enough to say it is worthwhile to learn about, but we are still largely unsure if it directly helps your business in an efficient manner.

Third level feeders
Magazines, websites, seminars. Getting a complete view of a technology can be further validated by reading trade magazines and major news websites.

The reason I say "major" news sites is that if the technology has the ability to bubble all the way up to a mainstream news outlet, it is probably worth taking a moment to evaluate.

What I consider major news sites are:
CNN.com
NYTimes.com
Yahoo.com
HuffingtonPost.com
Bloomberg.com
NPR.org

The *New York Times* is an interesting example. Usually, it will print most of its stories in its newspaper, spreading the concept even further and solidifying the concept that the technology is mainstream.

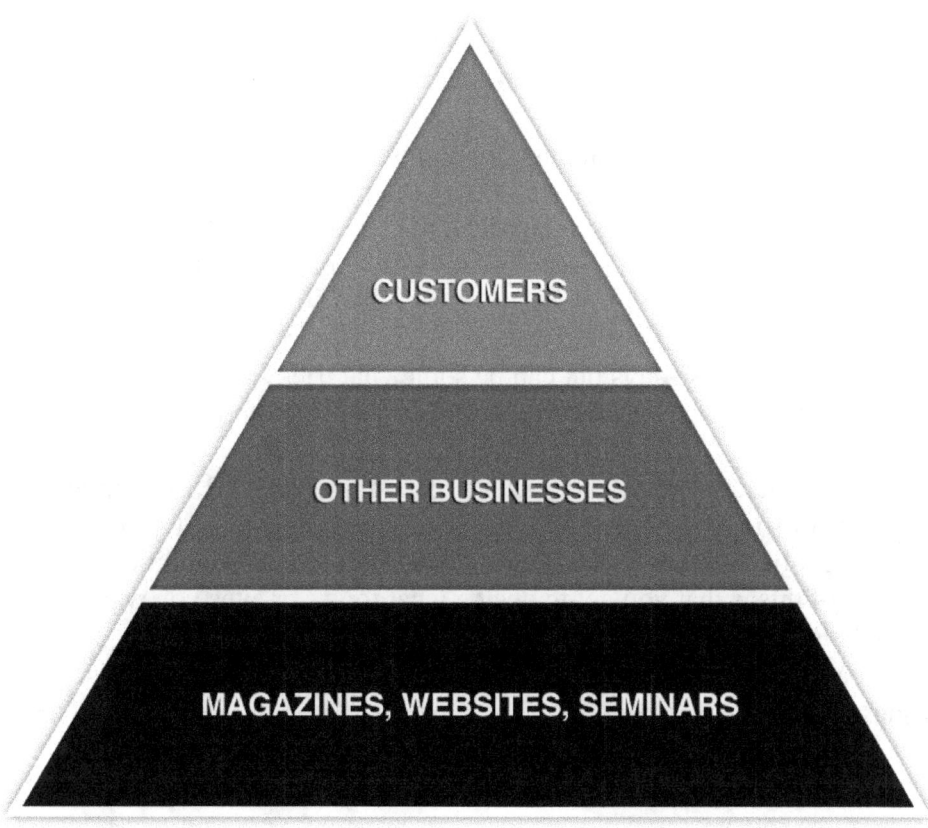

Exhibit 20. Information feeder tiers.

Three types of feeders for information. Start at the top and work your way down. As you go further down the pyramid, the relevancy of the information for you directly may be diluted.

Now you have a basic system for gathering information and sifting through it on a daily basis.

Realistically, you may not be able to ask these questions every day, and you certainly don't want to ask all of your customers.

What I recommend is that you spend at least thirty minutes a month asking these questions. Will you miss the latest and hottest trend? Maybe, but that is OK. If the trend is so hot that it burns out by the time you ask your questions, you didn't miss anything at all.

Think about it. For the past few decades, magazines told us once a month what the newest and greatest thing was, and that was totally sufficient. Tech certainly moves faster these days, but implementing this technology in the real business world has not evolved that much. People still take time and make calculated decisions. Your dollars are precious. Don't chase every new technology that comes around the corner.

As suggested in the earlier chapters of this book, if you do want to test out a new technology or invest in something, make sure you have a goal and a metric!

If you'd like to spend more time learning about the latest and greatest, I would recommend using some of the following tools and have them deliver summaries to your e-mail in-box. If you find yourself ignoring the e-mails, just turn off the service and go back to talking to your customers. They will always be more relevant!

Online feeders

Online tools are quite flexible these days but can be somewhat tricky to set up the first time around. This is not meant to be exhaustive, but it is a short list of awesome technologies.

- Google Reader. Google Reader uses a technology called RSS to gather data from various websites and places it in one simple page for you. Think of it like reading a newspaper's headlines first. The additional benefit of this is that you get to decide what topics or sites you want Google Reader to aggregate. The service itself is free.
- Flipboard. This is an app that works with iPhone, iPad, and Android.
- Industry-specific newsletters.

Summary

Openly ask for information from your customers. Verify it. Re-verify it. Test with a goal.

Chapter 9 - The Quest for Perfection

The surest hindrance of success is to have too high a standard of refinement in our own minds, or too high an opinion of the judgment of the public. He who is determined not to be satisfied with anything short of perfection will never do anything.
—Unknown

People like perfect.

But the reality is that perfection is a highly subjective term. It means different things to different people, and it may even change over time.

People think perfection is necessary since there are potential penalties associated with being less than perfect.

"I could lose money."
"It won't look exactly the way I imagined."
"My competitor's site will be stronger."
"But it doesn't do X, and I think that was a really cool idea."

For a moment, let's look at the other side of the coin.

Since your technology is an extension of your brand, you owe it to your brand to make your tech as strong as possible.

However, in real life, we have time and money constraints. Striving for perfection will cost you more in terms of money and time. I am not saying it is the wrong thing to do, but technology is largely imperfect. It is OK to approach technology in steps.

As mentioned earlier in this book, being able to cut some features and get something live is highly important. With a project that never goes live, you never get real customer feedback. This feedback is your perfection, since you are really building a product for your customers, not you. Focusing on real learning versus assumptions is how to make a better product or service.

Could you lose money if the technology product is not perfect? It is a debatable question.

You lose money when you ignore basic QA and your system doesn't work at all. If a user is not able to find your website or app, can't load it, or can't get basic info like your phone number or address, then you will lose money.

Once again, if you look at the Old School Simple technology pyramid, failing at the lower levels could spell disaster. Failing at the bottom levels directly correlates to frustrating your customers and not letting them fulfill their basic needs. Perfection may very well be a gradient scale. Perfection at the bottom of the Old School Simple pyramid is necessary and cannot be compromised. Perfection at the top when offering optional features is not required.

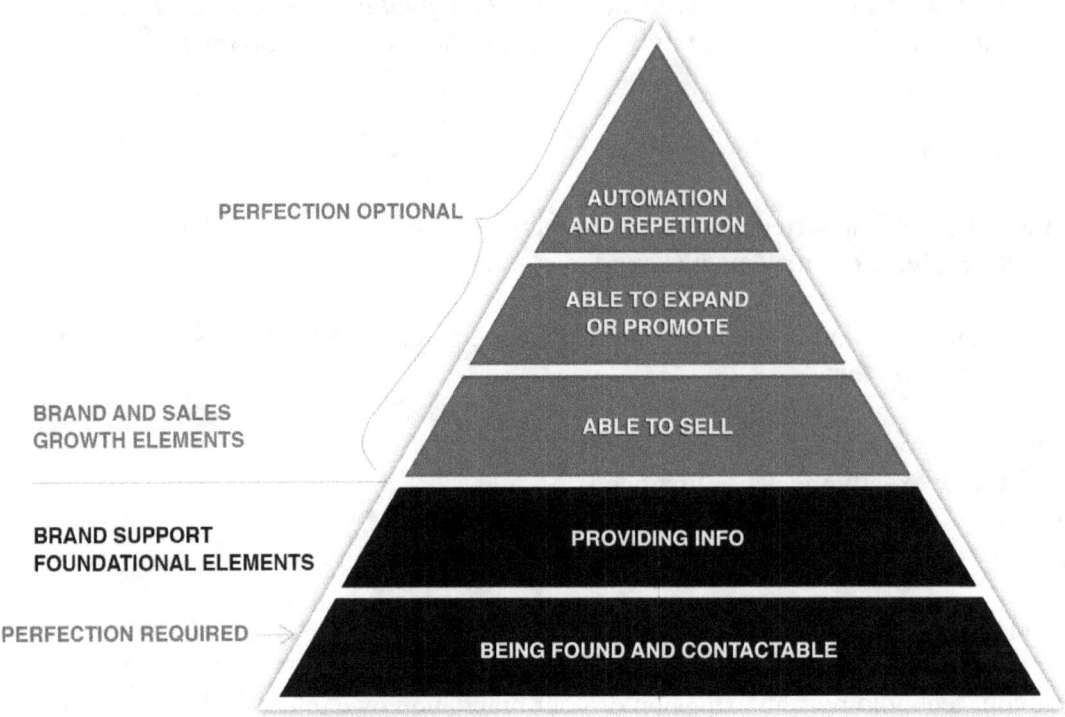

Exhibit 21. Old School Simple's pyramid and where perfection is required.

As long as your system is usable, your customers will usually work with you to help build it up. But always remember, technology is anchored by a quality product or service that keeps customers involved with your brand.

Summary

Depending on the type of project you are attempting, it is important to set quality standards for the team. Make sure you dedicate some time for quality assurance testing!

Chapter 10 - Identifying Fads

Movies are a fad. Audiences really want to see live actors on stage.
—Charlie Chaplin

Fads are one of the scariest things in the technology world and are equally scary for small business owners.

The simple fact is that it is easy to invest in something that will not be there in six months.

I often asked myself, how do I know if X is a fad or not?

Then I started to realize that my success rate was quite low when it came to identifying a fad. There were several reasons for this.

First, my decision process was very much colored by reading too much news that was often hype or PR. Of course, the technology sounded amazing; I was reading sales material, essentially.

Second, I tried to make a decision in a vacuum. I wasn't asking other people from varying demographic groups what they thought. I also wasn't observing how people were using the technology. I assumed too much.

Third, I personally wanted it to succeed so I could say I knew about it "way early."

Fourth, I didn't look at it from a revenue perspective—was anyone making any money off of this technology?

Fifth, I didn't see what the learning curve was. Often, the technology was complicated, even for a twenty-year-old, and introduced a unique lexicon to sound cool or new. In reality, it was just complicated.

Actually, spotting a fad is easy. It is all about waiting.

Take your time making a decision with technology. Identifying lasting technologies is really related to a few simple key indicators:

- The technology is simple, useful, and is easily integrated into daily life for a consumer and/or business.
- If you wait six months or a year, the money making opportunity within the technology still exists or has become better.
- Customers across a wide swath of demographics are actively using it. It is mainstream, in other words, and your customers actively voice concerns or frustrations that they can't utilize the technology with your business.

Can you add some other ways to measure if something is a fad? Yes, of course.

But the fact is that waiting is usually one of the most cost-effective strategies around.

For example, lets take a look at the Apple iPad. Many people would say it is the future of computing and no longer a fad.

Let's take this apart a bit.

It is undeniable that Apple has been massively successful selling the iPad. It is one of the fastest-selling electronic devices ever.

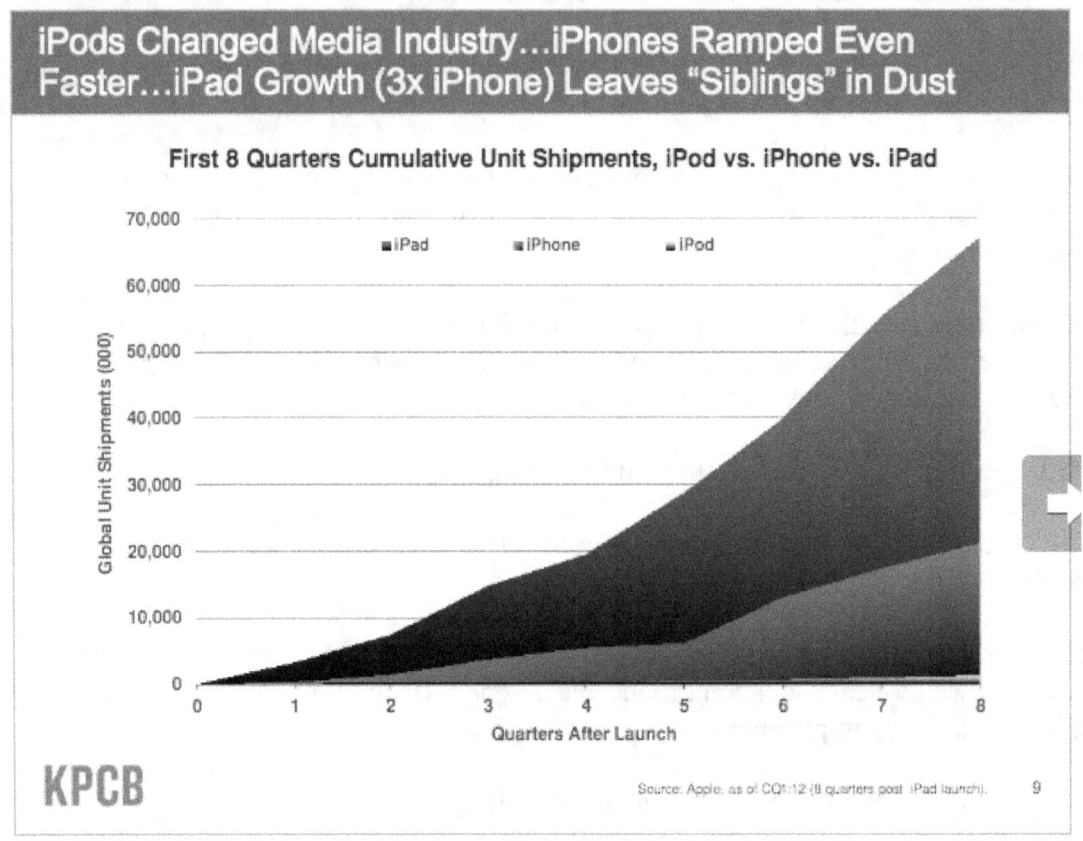

Exhibit 22. KPCB presentation by Mary Meeker, "Internet Trends," May 2012.

However, you are a small business owner. Is this technology relevant to you?

Even though the iPad has sold so many units, people still use regular desktops and notebook computers to access the Internet. Depending on the type of business you have, you might be seeing zero percent of people interacting with your business from a mobile device, or you might see 40 percent of your audience being mobile.

From a small business perspective, knowing more about how this technology affects you specifically can help you define if it is a fad for you.

Even though the iPad is widely known, there is still a large number of people who do not own one, have never used one, and potentially cannot afford one. These things are keeping the device somewhat exclusive and not universally understood.

I do think that the iPad will continue to grow, but it will take some more time before it is truly ubiquitous. If it gets to the point of being ubiquitous and does not get overtaken by another new technology, we can safely say it is no longer a fad.

If we go back to our original statement, the iPad is growing rapidly, for sure, but it has a lot farther to go before it mandates our attention and investment.

The real question still abounds: Will you lose anything by waiting?

Yes, you are losing a portion of the risk associated with being on the cutting edge. This is actually a gain for you. Creating a scenario with a higher likelihood of success is important for any business but especially for a small business with limited resources. In other words, waiting is part of the strategy.

Summary

The tech world is full of fads. Given the speed at which the tech world moves, if you wait six to twelve months, you can usually spot a fad.

Section II - DEFINE

By now, you as a business owner have quite a few notes about your goals, your history, and a more rounded view on brand development.

I want to start to build on this foundation knowledge by beefing up your understanding of the technology world and giving you skills to interact with technology professionals.

I want to help you understand the technology landscape or playing field so you understand what you are getting into to. Part of this is to arm you with the skills and knowledge to avoid being scammed. Believe it or not, people out there will gladly take your money and not provide you with a finished product or a product at all.

At this point, I would like to give you a few guides which you can use over and over in your business. These guides are really focused on finding and implementing technology in your business.

The following guides are included:
1) Technology definitions – so you can understand and conceptualize options available to you.
2) RFP or Request For Proposal – this helps you gather proposals for your tech project and helps you map out the objective of your tech project. Think of it like a mini-business plan.
3) Job descriptions – I wrote up sample job descriptions for hiring a web developer and web agency.
4) Tips and tricks for interviewing and managing technology team members
5) Sample contracts for hiring a technology team member or agency.
6) Reflection questions – simple questions to help you understand what went well and what could have been improved upon.
7) Lastly, a simple checklist to sum up the Ask Define Measure methodology.

All of these guides will also be available on my website. http://OldSchoolSimple.com

Chapter 11 - The Obligatory Facebook Chapter

The thing that we are trying to do at Facebook, is just help people connect and communicate more efficiently. Mark Zuckerberg, CEO of Facebook

Social media is very popular these days. It's people connecting to people, people connecting to companies, and people connecting to products. The conversations are somewhat public, and the underlying concept is that sharing information amongst groups helps everyone.

There are several social networks out there. The biggest by far is Facebook. Some others you may have heard of are Twitter, Google+, Foursquare, Tumblr, and Pinterest. This list frequently changes, but consider these the giants of the industry at the moment.

Each network has its features and user bases. You also may see the same person on several networks. This is a result of no single network offering best-in-class for all of its features. People always want to be on top of everything, and there are certainly social media junkies who are on every platform. These junkies usually see social media as a full-time job, and some even turn it into a career.

In general, social media is a great place to share ideas and potentially have a two-way conversation.

Now you are probably wondering, "Why do I need to have a conversation online when I can converse with my customers in real life?"

The advantage is that you can talk to customers who don't live near you or who do business with you online only. Another advantage is that the conversations themselves are stored online so that other people can read them and hopefully get some value from them. And yet another advantage is that your conversation doesn't have to be text; it can be a video, a photo, or any digital media.

For the purposes of this book, I wanted to give you a very broad description of how Facebook works, but, more importantly, how most people use it. The information here is pretty consistent across all the social networks; however, each network has its own nuances.

What is Facebook?

Facebook is a social platform/network. What does that mean? Well, it means that Facebook is not just one site anymore. It allows users to be on the network generating new data/conversations/interactions, even when they are on other websites.

Facebook has a technology that allows people to "share" or "like" other pieces of content on the web and have them show up on Facebook.com. The actual area where this will appear seems to change daily due to various upgrades Facebook makes but the most common place these likes show up is on the user's page and within the newsfeed.

Each user has his or her own page where all of their interactions are stored in what is called a timeline. The timeline is just like any other timeline, noting when, where, who, what, and potentially why you interacted with something. It is a running history of your life, in some ways.

Each user on Facebook connects to other users by being "friends" with them. Your friends get to interact with you, see your updates, and send updates to you. These groups of friends are meant to mimic real-life groups of friends. The biggest difference is that most people call lots of different people friends. Friends can range from your closest companions to people you've met only once.

Facebook's home page contains a feature called the "feed" or "news feed," which is where all the updates, interactions, and content relevant to you appears in one constantly updating stream of information. The feed allows you to see updates all day long from the people you are associated with. Depending on the number of friends you have, the stream can be quite a fire hose of information. If you have a lot of friends that are active users on Facebook, the news feed is inundated with all the various updates that are being made.

Exhibit 23. A feed is a central pipeline. KPCB presentation by Mary Meeker, "Internet Trends," May 2012.

Facebook is also completely accessible via mobile phone or tablet. About 50 percent of users access Facebook by a mobile device and regular computer.

How does Facebook make money?

Facebook primarily makes money through advertising. It sells ads in various locations throughout the site. Anyone with a credit card and an offer can purchase ads with

Facebook. The real power of these ads comes from the targeting that Facebook offers. It allows you to target by age, gender, location, marital status, interests, education level, etc. The most powerful element in this list is "interests." Facebook has been able to catalog you as a user and define what your interests are and, in some cases, knows more about you than you do yourself.

For all users on Facebook, the site is currently free.

Who uses Facebook?

As of May 2012, there are around 845 million users on Facebook, according to its recently filed S1. (The S1 is a document required by the Securities and Exchange Commission prior to going public. It details out the company business model, risks and details of the public offering.)

Given that there are so many people on it, it is safe to say that pretty much every demographic type is on Facebook.

The site is accessible from almost every country in the world, with some exceptions, like China, where it is banned for the most part.

Age-wise, you see people from thirteen all the way up to one hundred on Facebook. People under thirteen are technically not allowed to use the site.

What do most people do on Facebook?
The main activities on Facebook are viewing what your friends are doing via the news feed, looking at/uploading photos, playing games, and chatting. People's usage models on a mobile device versus a desktop are relatively similar, however, I would argue that less people play Facebook games on their mobile device at the moment. I suspect that this will change by the end of 2012. One big difference with mobile usage is the concept of checking in. When a user checks in on Facebook, the mobile device creates an update on Facebook saying where you are, potentially whom you are with, and what you are doing.

Facebook's primary concept is to help people communicate more. It is debatable if the communication is more effective but it certainly does increase the amount of communication out there these days. People can communicate via photos, videos, and text making Facebook a rather engaging experience.

Facebook has become somewhat of a rant outlet that can create a lot of negative publicity for businesses. It has become common practice that if you have had a bad experience with a business, you rant or complain about it on Facebook to all of your friends. Some people who have had a very bad experience may ask their friends to not go to that business but most of the time people are just venting.

As a large business, there are tools to monitor what is being said about your company but as a small business with limited resources and time, it is better to focus on providing consistently high quality service.

How do other small businesses use Facebook?

There are three main ways that small businesses use Facebook currently. There are certainly more options available, but these tend to be the ones people are most familiar with.

First, small businesses advertise on Facebook to find new customers. You have to set up your own ads in Facebook, so a little bit of technical knowledge is required. You also need to be good at writing engaging ad copy. Small businesses seem to have varying levels of success with Facebook advertising. Some find it too expensive, some find it too hard to manage, but some do amazingly well. There are several books out there about how to advertise on Facebook, so I won't get into that topic. But be wary of buying these books, since the Facebook platform itself changes often, and the books are frequently out of date. Get them from your library to save money.

Second, small businesses try to handle customer service on Facebook. Often, people will talk on Facebook about a positive or negative experience with a particular brand. People have become lazy and do not go to your corporate website anymore to send you feedback privately. Many prefer to make their comments public now. This can be good and bad.

A common example of this is when people have a bad experience with an airline or the airline loses their bag and they post about it on Facebook, sharing it with all of their friends. This is bad for the airline's brand if not addressed. The airline may have the ability to interact with this consumer on Facebook and try to make things right. There are also several books on handling customer service issues on Facebook. My personal opinion is that people feel less sympathetic to large corporations on Facebook versus the small mom-and-pop business around the corner. As a small business, I urge you to provide great customer service every day. Your reputation is not just in your neighborhood anymore; it is now online for the world to see.

The third way small businesses use Facebook is to gain "fans." Lets say you run Joe's Deli. Joe's Deli sets up a brand page on Facebook and asks people to "like" the page. Once a person likes the page, they are considered a fan. Joe's Deli can now communicate directly with that fan. In other words, liking or being a fan of a brand is giving the brand permission to interact with you. Most brands take advantage of this permission by sending consumers photo updates or coupons, asking questions, or including them in other marketing campaigns. This virtual conversation is what Facebook is all about.

Take a moment to think about Facebook's core feature. It allows people to talk to their friends and the businesses they like. Both of these things can be done with zero technology.

Facebook's value really comes from the history it collects and its ability to advertise to you.

Summary

Facebook is a platform to help businesses—large and small—communicate with their consumers. Is there more to learn about Facebook? Yes, there is a ton more, but hopefully this gives you the basics so when your friends and family discuss Facebook, you won't feel left out.

A very important question to ask yourself is "should I invest time and money into Facebook?" I would advise that you should experience Facebook but for you to invest money, I would make sure you have a goal and a metric before spending anything. Also, ask yourself, "am I getting the most out of my customer conversations currently?"

Chapter 12 - Current Technologies and Major Caveats

In fact, technology has been the story of human progress from as long back as we know. In 100 years people will look back on now and say, 'That was the Internet Age.' And computers will be seen as a mere ingredient to the Internet Age. – Reed Hastings, CEO of Netflix

Before we jump into what small business media technologies are currently available, I am going to fall back on creating a decision matrix for you.

First, we need to figure out a bit more about your personality. Why do you care about these new technologies?

- Do you want to be at the forefront of technology?
- Do you want to know where everyone else is?
- Do you want to catch up?
- Are you scared of what you are missing?
- Do you think you are losing money by not using these technologies?
- Do you want to see if these technologies can cut costs?
- Are you afraid your brand is becoming stale or old?
- Do you want to become rich overnight?

All of the questions above identify fears rooted in basic human characteristics.

Humans cluster around common ideas, likes, and dislikes. We also naturally follow leaders. This is usually first manifested when you want to be friends with the popular kid. We hope to become popular just by association.

Sometimes this works, but a lot of times it doesn't. The core reason it doesn't work very well is because the cool kid's endorsement can only be given out a limited number of times before it becomes worthless.

In the online world, the more people group or cluster around a particular technology, the more legitimate it becomes. However, as the masses adopt a technology, the early adopters tend to move on to the next evolution. This cycle happens extremely quickly compared to what happens in real life. Part of the reason that technology innovation happens so fast is that there is a monetary incentive to steal the other person's audience and get as many eyeballs as you possibly can. This is partially fostered by investors, but I will save that discussion for another book.

The big question is, which technologies do we pay attention to and which ones do we ignore?

It is usually very hard to be an early adopter and get your bets 100 percent right. It is much easier to be a late adopter, especially if you have limited resources.

Imagine the folks who started buying advertising on Facebook in 2007, when it was first starting to grow rapidly. Those folks made a tremendous amount of money very quickly. The people entering Facebook advertising in 2012 have a much more defined platform to work with, but it may prove harder to make a profit since there is more competition and more professionals on the system.

Most people would read the above paragraph and think they missed out big-time. What most small business owners don't see is that the advertisers who entered early in 2007 were professionals. They had very specific metrics, large budgets, and their sole job was to create advertisements.

The reality is that you didn't miss out on anything. You let other people spend their money and create a solid system for you. The professionals and early adopters paid to have the bugs worked out.

But back to the original question, why should you care about these new technologies?

There are only two reasons you should care about new technology:

- Your customers are asking you en masse to be there. They are somewhat frustrated that they cannot find you there. Listen to them and join.
- You are blocking people from spending money with you. The majority likes your product, but there are too many speed bumps to buy your product.

Now, if we look at the statements above, neither of them is focused on being first. It's about the consumer. The customer, at the end of the day, should be creating technology opportunities for you. It will ultimately be your decision if you want to go forward with the opportunity or not. You have tons of customers who are constantly testing and evaluating new technology. The community naturally decides what is cool, and that information can flow back to you for free.

The key is to frequently ask what they are doing with their technology.

You shouldn't have to hire a technology consultant to tell you what is new. You have free consultants come into your shop every day who are willing to tell you what is new.

With the speed at which technology moves, it is virtually impossible to stay on top of every new thing that comes out. But if there is an instance where your customers get frustrated or have an experience that is not in line with your brand, this will create a negative image of your brand long-term.

For example, have you been to a website that looks like it was designed back in 1995? It loads slowly and has flashing colors and grainy images? All of a sudden, a brand you thought was cool became antiquated.

Today, if I try to access a website on a mobile device and it takes forever to load or doesn't work at all, it becomes a frustrating experience.

One major key to technology decisions is to make sure your decisions don't frustrate your core customers.

In this chapter, we are focusing on broad groups of technologies so you can have a conversation about them with your programmer or customers. The information is aimed at giving you foundational-level knowledge. If you consider yourself more than just a novice, feel free to skip ahead. If you want a quick refresher, skim over the information below.

The text is written in layperson's language in homage to my dad, who always asked me to explain these terms. Most tech experts will say the definitions could use refinement, which is true, but this is the quick and dirty version.

Basic technologies terms

Device - A device can be anything from a desktop computer, mobile phone, or a tablet, to a game console or TV. The easy way to think of it is anything that has a computer chip in it and connects to another system for information.

URL/domain - A URL or domain is essentially your address on the Internet. Most commonly, domains are represented like this: http://www.AustinDeli.com. The http://www. is a standard protocol that tells the computer how to talk to the website. For the purposes of this book, you don't have to worry too much about this. The point of URLs is that they are an easy way for humans to remember where your website is located. Anyone can purchase a domain.

CPU - A CPU is the brain of a computer or device. It technically stands for central processing unit. Without the brain, the device won't work, just like without your brain, you won't function.

E-mail - E-mail, or electronic mail, is a standard way of sending written communication online. To send or receive an e-mail, you must have an e-mail address. Your e-mail address should be associated with your domain, for instance, krish@austindeli.com. The @ symbol is read as "at" and is necessary when addressing an e-mail to someone.

Instant messaging - Instant messaging usually refers to a program that allows you to send quick text messages back and forth between a list of friends. The main difference between instant messaging and e-mail is that the programs are usually running on your desktop and can interrupt what you are doing currently. In contrast, e-mail will only be seen if you open your e-mail program or website.

SMS - A SMS (short message system) or text message can be thought of as a short e-mail, in some ways. The main difference is that it was originally designed for mobile phones. It allows phones to send text messages in a standard format very quickly.

Video chat - Video chat is a technology that allows you to talk to one other person or a group of people using the camera in your computer. The conversation flows exactly like an in-person conversation. To have a video chat, you usually need a program like Skype.

Podcast - A podcast is simply a talk by one person or between many people that is recorded and able to be played back on a portable music player, like an iPod.

iPod – An iPod is a device made by Apple which was originally designed as a music player only. It is largely credited with revolutionizing the music industry for the digital world. It works solely with Apple's iTunes platform and store which is an online media store.

MP3 – A MP3 is a file format that is specific to audio. Older audio files used to be rather large but with the advent of the MP3, the file sizes became much smaller and allowed users to store many more songs on devices like the iPod. The format compresses audio and may actually lose some of the audio quality to achieve smaller file sizes. It is widely considered the standard of music and electronics industry these days.

Web browser - A web browser is a program that allows you to access web pages on the Internet. There are many types of browsers, including Internet Explorer, Firefox, Google Chrome, Safari, Opera, etc.

App - An app, or application, is like a cross between a website and a software program. Most people use the term to refer to various applications on their mobile devices. Some examples are games like Angry Birds, or the Facebook app. Apps allow you to take advantage of not only web features, but new interfaces, like a touch screen or a device that tracks your physical movement.

Hardware/software - Hardware is any technology you can physically touch, like a computer, phone, tablet, server, etc. Hardware as a term refers not only to the device but also any component in the device itself, like the chips, boards, circuits, etc. Software, on the other hand, usually refers to a computer program. This can be something like Microsoft Office, which you install on a computer but you can't physically touch.

File formats

PDF - PDF stands for Portable Document Format. Consider it a picture of a document in its simplest form. You can see the document and it looks exactly like the original, but you usually can't edit it unless you have special permissions. This is a great format for contracts or documents where formatting is important.

DOC - A doc usually refers to a Microsoft Word document. For instance, if you type a letter in Word and save it, you will end up with a doc. In some versions of Word, you may end up with a docx, which is essentially the same thing.

XLS - XLS usually refers to a file in Microsoft Excel, which is a spreadsheet program. It may also be referred to as an XLSX document.

PPT or deck - PPT or deck usually refers to a Microsoft PowerPoint file. PowerPoint is presentation software that allows you to make presentation slides.

ODF - ODF stands for Open Document Format. This is similar to a MS Word doc, but is the standard used by Google Docs and OpenOffice. It can be opened in MS Word.

Picture formats

There are tons of picture file formats out there. Frankly, it doesn't make sense to know the nuances of each file format. The most important thing to know is what they are called. Here are the most popular ones:

- JPEG
- TIFF
- GIF
- PNG

About 90 percent of images will use one of the above formats. All of these can be opened in most web browsers and they can be opened on both a Mac and PC.

Social technologies

Here is a quick list of the biggest and most influential social media sites as of mid-2012.

Facebook - Facebook is a community of around 900 million people across the globe. It allows for messaging, picture sharing, business pages, etc. It is the largest social network in the world.

Twitter - Twitter is a short messaging platform using SMS that limits messages to one hundred forty characters. It is a micro blogging service that lets users post text and link to anything on the web.

Google+ -Google+ is the social platform developed by Google in 2011. It has many of the features of Facebook and Twitter but ties together many Google properties, like YouTube, Google Search, and other sites.

Foursquare - Foursquare allows a person to share their physical location by "checking in." It helped popularize gamification by rewarding people (with badges or, in some cases, coupons and discounts from the establishment where a user is located) for checking in. Gamification, in case you are wondering is when a regular task is turned into a game, with game mechanics, game theory and game theory. An old game that most cereal producers used was to collect box tops for a prize. This allowed them to sell you more cereal without resorting to an obvious push.

Tumblr - Tumblr is a blog platform and social network where users can post original content, as well as curate content they enjoy.

Specific website technologies

HTML - HTML is one of the most prolific technical languages on the Internet. Almost every web page uses HTML in some format today. It is a very structured language that every programmer must know. Knowing how to read HTML can be a very useful skill as a client. Consider HTML a common language on the Internet.

CSS - CSS stands for cascading style sheets. CSS works in conjunction with HTML to help you format your website. A lot of the design parameters—like font size, color, and other attributes—can be stored once in this sheet and referred to in the HTML. This allows your HTML to look a bit cleaner and you can make multiple changes by simply changing one parameter in one location.

API – An API is an application programming interface. It allows two systems to talk to each other in a structured format. Think of it like if you had two business people meeting, one is from France and the other is from Malaysia. They decide to use English as the common language to conduct business.

CMS – A CMS is a Content Management System. A CMS is like a refrigerator; it allows you to store a variety of ingredients, or content, in one central place. Based on what the user wants at any particular time, specific ingredients are called to create a web page. In your refrigerator, you might have ingredients to make a cheeseburger, and those same ingredients can make a grilled cheese sandwich—two different outcomes with similar ingredients.

A content management system is a way of managing your online content, including pictures, text, website layout etc. Some of the more popular CMS systems are WordPress, Joomla and Drupal. These systems allow you to put up a website within a few hours and allow for almost instant blogging functionality. The best part about these systems is the community around them. Often times you can find help from another user or find add-ons for your website through this community. Each CMS is quite unique so if you start with WordPress, the add ons you get for it will not work with a Drupal site. Take this into consideration when approaching your developers or your long-term road map.

Guidelines – There are several organizations that provide guidelines on how things should look on the web but here are some of the most important and influential.

W3C – The W3C is the World Wide Web Consortium, it sets forth a set of standards for the web with the focus being on compatibility and accessibility for all types of people.   The W3C helps define rules around HTML usage and other technology protocols.

ADA – American Disabilities Act – (http://en.wikipedia.org/wiki/Americans_with_Disabilities_Act_of_1990) - This act set forth standards and laws for how technology should be designed to ensure people of all abilities can access it. If you design a website, you should take into consideration people who might be vision impaired.   A good description of how a person with disabilities may access the internet can be found here. It also details out the web specific guidelines set forth by the ADA - http://www.ada.gov/websites2.htm.

IAB – The Internet Advertising Bureau is a group that is comprised of various advertising organizations. It helps set standards for ad unit sizes, and works with regulators around how online advertising should work.

Major platforms

Before we talk about major platforms, it is important to understand what an operating system is. An operating system is the basic set of rules that a computer uses to work with the hardware and other software programs. Think of it like a human language. If you speak English, everything you read or interact with should be in English. Platforms are essentially branded operating systems and are somewhat walled gardens meaning. Most platforms don't play nice with each other forcing engineers to build variations of the same product. This creates additional costs for the small business owner in the long run but also enables them to get in front of more potential customers.

Apple Mac - Apple is a computer company that started back in the 1970s. Its computers are often referred to as Macs. Macs use similar hardware to PCs but require different software to operate correctly. A PC is a general term used for a personal computer but is more commonly used to describe non-Apple computers.

iPhone and iPad - An iPhone is a smartphone that allows people to not only make calls, but watch videos, listen to music, use apps, and access the Internet. Phones that only allow for calling and messaging are called feature phones. It is made by Apple and uses the proprietary iOS operating system. iPad is a tablet device that uses the iOS operating system also and the same touch interface as the iPhone. A tablet computer does not have a keyboard like a traditional laptop. iPad is also made by Apple.

Windows - Windows is an operating system made by Microsoft for PCs. It is currently the dominant operating system in the world. Windows introduced a whole new lexicon to the world that helped computer users store and open files within windows on their computer.

Windows Mobile - Windows Mobile is Microsoft's operating system for its smartphones and tablets. It has many of the same features as the desktop version but is optimized for a touch interface instead of a keyboard.

Android - Android is Google's mobile operating system, which competes directly with Apple's iOS. Android can be installed on a variety of smartphones. It also takes advantage of a touch interface and integrates many Google products, like YouTube, Google Maps, and Google Search. It allows for third party apps too.

Third-Party Apps – within the computer world, a wide range of companies can develop applications or apps. Many times the company who develops the core operating system may also design the applications. An example of this is when Microsoft makes Windows and also makes Microsoft Word to run on Windows. Companies like Microsoft and Apple also make it possible for other companies to develop applications to run on their operating systems. In the case of Apple, they actively encourage developers to design apps for their phones and tablet devices. These apps that are not designed internally are considered 3rd party apps. Since the core platform company does not make them, the user risks installing something that may not always work correctly.

Software languages

I debated writing this section since it is virtually impossible to explain these technologies without confusing the layperson. For the most part, it is good to know these terms but you don't have to fully understand how each technology works as a small business owner.

Flash - Flash is a technology owned by Adobe. It allows websites to present video, audio, and interactivity online. Think of it like an interactive comic book online. Flash is not supported by Apple mobile devices, so your customers may not be able to see your website properly if you include Flash and they use an iPhone or iPad.

JavaScript - JavaScript is a scripting language that can be embedded in HTML. It essentially adds interactivity to pages. For a more in-depth description, visit http://www.w3schools.com/js/js_intro.asp. To clarify, a script is a series of instructions that a computer must do in order to achieve an outcome. Think of it like a highly structured task list.

Java - Java is a programming language originally developed by Sun Microsystems. It is used extensively online and in games. It is technically open-source software as of 2006.

PHP - PHP is a scripting language. It allows a website to think and give a specific answer based on your inputs. For instance, if a user enters in X value, the site will provide Y answer.

Ruby on Rails - Ruby on Rails is a relatively new programming language that uses the Model-View-Controller framework or MVC. This allows the programmer to interact with multiple parts of a website from one simpler coding platform. For more info, please go here: http://ruby.about.com/od/rubyonrails/a/whatisrails.htm.

C++ - C++ is one of the oldest programming languages around, dating back to 1983. It is an object-based language that is very widely used today.

Hardware

Servers - A server is a computer that is usually dedicated to hosting your website. It is always on and allows people to access your website from anywhere in the world. A server is essentially where your website lives in the world. Servers are usually directly connected to the Internet unless they have specific security restrictions.

Handset - A handset is another term for a phone or smartphone. It refers to the actual device you hold in your hands.

Modem – For most people the modem is the little device that sits in between your computer and the physical connection to your Internet, usually a phone wire or cable wire. This device simply helps get information from the Internet and to the internet from your computer devices.

Router – A router is a device that you install between your modem and your computer devices. It allows for several devices to share one Internet connection.

Hard Disk Drive (HDD) – a hard drive is a type of memory for your computer that is considered to be somewhat permanent. The information you save on your hard drive is not erased when you turn off the computer. Hard drives these days are made from a mix of discs or chips. The drives which are made from discs do have moving parts while the ones with chips do not have any moving parts.

Touch Screen – most computer screens require a mouse or keyboard to interact with them. These days, more and more devices are allowing for you to touch them. Touch screens are very popular within the smartphone and tablet market. As a small business owner it is important to ask your designers and developers to take this into consideration when implementing new technology.

Networking

Wi-Fi - Wi-Fi is a general term used for wireless Internet access. It requires a Wi-Fi-enabled device and a Wi-Fi router to work.

3G - 3G is a cellular technology that helps transfer data to your mobile device wirelessly. It is actually a series of radio frequencies and was made available publicly around 2001. It allowed for many innovations in the smartphone market.

4G - 4G is also a cellular technology that helps transfer data on mobile devices at a much faster speed than 3G. Marketing and standards for 4G vary from network to network and country to country. Some 4G networks are as fast as wired connections.

Broadband - Broadband is a reference to a wired Internet connection that is faster than a regular phone-based modem. Phone-based modems used to top out around 56 kilobytes per second. Broadband speeds today greatly exceed that and continue to get faster and faster. The larger the broadband rate, the more data can be transferred quickly. This enables people to send and receive large files—like video, music, and other documents—quickly.

Fiber - Fiber refers to optical fiber, which, instead of using copper wire to transmit data, uses glass fiber and light. The advantage is that the wires are usually smaller and can carry data much faster. The downside is that most of the data transmission infrastructure—in the US, at least—is copper-based and the roll-out of fiber has been slow due to costs.

Cable - Cable refers to the copper cable wire you usually get your TV signal from. Cable TV providers have been able to use their larger cables to transmit Internet signals and TV signals at the same time.

DSL - DSL stands for Digital Subscriber Line. This technology allows regular phone wires or POTS (Plain Old Telephone System) lines to transmit data at broadband speeds. The DSL technology is limited in terms of speed and tends to be slower the farther away you are from the phone network itself. DSL enables you to get faster internet with regular phone lines.

Jargon and buzzwords

It seems like every day there is a new vocabulary in the technology world. Guess what? The vast majority of these new terms or buzzwords are easily simplified into layperson's terms.

Here are some of the most popular words that firms tend to throw around. My advice is that if you hear or read these terms in a proposal, make sure you clarify what these mean. Unfortunately, with most buzzwords, people have different interpretations of the term.

SEO Optimized – Often times designers or web developers may say that a site is SEO optimized without knowing what that really means. SEO stands for search engine optimized which is set of theories and principles that is supposed to help your website be found on search engines like Google, Bing and Yahoo! There are certainly some basic things you can do to help your website be found on the search engines but this is a very dynamic industry where the rules often change. SEO is not a one time event, it is important to remember it is an ongoing process.

Bug - Bug is a term used to describe something that is broken in a technology or design product. If you go to a website and an image doesn't show up, that can be considered a bug.

Open source - This term is becoming increasingly popular within the tech community these days. Open source usually refers to the licensing around software. Ten to twenty years ago, if a company wrote a piece of code or software, they didn't want anyone outside the company to touch it or know how it was made. This allowed companies like Microsoft to make products and charge quite a bit of money for things like Microsoft Office, Microsoft Windows, etc. The money you paid for each product was a license to use it on your computer. With open source, the idea is that the code itself is made public in hopes that people add to it, make it stronger, and fix any issues. Usually the software is given away since no one technically owns it. In the past, people worried that if they got the open source version of something, they wouldn't have any support. This is partially true. You don't have a customer service number to call most of the time, but there are usually very robust online forums that will help you with most issues. Also, many businesses have built their revenue model around supporting open source software. In other words, they provide customization, technical support, and guidance. The key things to remember about open source are that it is free, open, and customizable.

Scalable - This is a term usually used extensively by engineering teams or investors. It refers to how well something can grow. Some web technologies are really meant for a small number of users and slow down quite a bit when lots of people use them at once. Think of this like trying to put ten people in a Honda Civic versus ten people in a Greyhound bus. The bus is inherently designed for larger groups and is able to move safely with dozens of people, while the Honda would be struggling to, first, fit that many people, and, second, drive safely. The vast majority of small businesses don't know if they need something scalable. That is OK. I would recommend starting with the smaller/easier solution first and see if you are attracting a lot of attention/users. If you are, there are lots of options to enhance the speed of your current platform without investing in a whole new platform. From a small business owner perspective, it may be important to plan for additional costs in terms of capacity or a full rebuild if your project scales quickly.

Future-proof - This is a marketing term. As you and I know, no one truly knows the future, so it is hard to say what we are "proofing" from. Some engineers will say that a system is future-proof, but in reality what they mean is that the code they are using is using current standards. This is a good thing, since current standards will usually create a solid base for future upgrades. However, there will be a time when you'll have to throw away most of what has been built and rebuild it using the new technology. Technology is like a car, in some ways. It has some planned obsolescence built into it.

Flexible - This is one of the trickiest terms out there. It can mean so many things. The word is used by technology teams and creative teams. It can mean that the layout of the site is easy to move around or the technology can talk to other systems or the site might automatically change based on the screen size viewing it. If your team says something is "flexible," ask them for specific examples of how it is flexible. It might also be good to find out what flexibility is requiring you to give up. When you try to accommodate many people and technologies, you may have to give up something. Find out what that might be.

Easy to use - Right now you are thinking, "Easy for you is way different than easy for me." Never take this comment at face value. When engineers tells you something is "easy," they are looking at it from their personal experience level. Since "easy to use" is such a subjective term, you might want the engineer to show you why he or she thinks it is easy and compare it to another system. The other way to do this is to ask the engineering team to allow you to test a sample system before committing.

WYSIWYG - What You See Is What You Get, pronounced "wizzy-wig," this is actually a slightly technical term, but what it refers to is the visual interface you use when entering data. In the past, when you wanted to enter text into a website, you had to edit the actual HTML code. Today's technologies allow you to enter text into an interface that looks similar to Microsoft Word or any other text editor. Essentially, what you type in is what it will look like on the web.

Shareable - Shareable is a term that became popular around 2007 or so when sites like Facebook became popular. People used to share via MySpace and e-mail, but Facebook specifically introduced a "share" button and coined the term "shareable." In layperson's terms, this is referring to something on your website that is worthy of sending to your friends via a social media site like Facebook or Twitter. Often, people like to share photos, videos, interesting news, links, etc. From an engineering perspective, what you are looking for is a way to make your content easier to share. This is usually in the form of one or many social media buttons.

Cloud - The cloud is a concept that allows you to store data on another computer (usually more than one) that is connected to the Internet. The benefits are that you don't need a giant computer hard drive to store all of your data and you will have access to the data from any device. It also protects you from computer theft in some ways, because if a person steals your computer, you still have your data somewhere else. For most small businesses, the cloud concept is not really that important right now. From a data security perspective, I would always recommend storing important files in the cloud, but it is not imperative.

Optimized - Many creative or engineering firms will say a technology product is "optimized." This term may mean different things for creative folks and engineering folks. From a creative perspective, this might mean the images are compressed and therefore load fast. From an engineering perspective, this might mean the files are compressed and the site looks consistent across many devices. It is important to clarify what this means and how you can test it. Also, optimization itself is a process; ask your developers to help optimize the site again six to twelve months down the road. There are always news ways springing up of tweaking things and making them faster.

Design Terms

UX – User Experience is a somewhat general term used these days to describe how a person access your website or app. It usually shows a path of how a person enters, completes an action and then leaves. Learning more about UX can enable you and your designers to reduce consumer stress when they are interacting with your products. The goal is to make it as easy as possible and to not force them to think too much!

A/B testing – The idea behind A/B testing is that you as the website owner should be constantly testing elements on your website. In certain instances you might change the color of your website, pictures, or the location of forms. Each of these changes has an impact on your user and will either make it easier or harder for them to complete an action. With the A/B test you can test the original version (A) versus the new version (B) and see which one performs better. It is called an A/B test since you are only testing one change at a time. If you change more than one thing at once, it is hard to say what caused the data to change. There is another school of thought around multi-variate testing, but that is usually more suited for sites with very high traffic levels and more robust analytics.

Use Cases – Use Cases are essentially documents that plot out what a user of your technology is intended to do and how they will accomplish it. For example, a user might want to order a sandwich from your deli. The use case would be oriented towards how they enter the site, pick the sandwich, process payment and get a confirmation. It is important to note what kind of errors the user might run into along this process.

Wireframes – If you think of a house blueprint, that is the same thing as a wireframe. It is a simplistic outline of what elements will go into a larger project. It shows placement, relative size and other key information. It does not show stylistic elements usually. The goal of the document is to quickly show how a website might work and give it a basic architecture. The document is incredibly helpful for designers and engineers. It works hand in hand with the use cases.

Summary

Technology terms are abundant—asking the engineer or designer to compare the term to a real world scenario will usually help you understand the technology.

Always ask questions if you don't understand a specific piece of technology.

Don't worry about remembering all of this. You can just bookmark these pages and refer back to them later on.

Lastly, I will continue to update this section via our website with links to helpful videos and/or simple explanations. It is almost guaranteed that this list will continue to grow.

Chapter 13 - Using an RFP to Find a Tech Provider

It's not going to get any easier. We've got to find a way to get it done.
—Unknown

One of the hardest things to do is actually find a company or person to help you with your tech project.

Usually the process of finding a tech provider is incredibly inefficient. It starts off with people searching online for terms like "website builder" or "website designer."

Given the number of ads on sites like Google for these general terms, it is hard to tell if a person or company is legitimate, mainly because you have never heard of that web development company before and you don't have a great way of verifying them. This chapter talks about getting them to respond to a request for proposal (RFP) that helps you evaluate them once you find them. But first we have to find the provider.

The other way people go about finding a tech provider or designer is to just ask their friends and family, saying, "Do you know anyone who can build a website?" You'll usually get referred a few times over and end up with some guy working out of his spare bedroom, a guy no one has vouched for, people just know he exists.

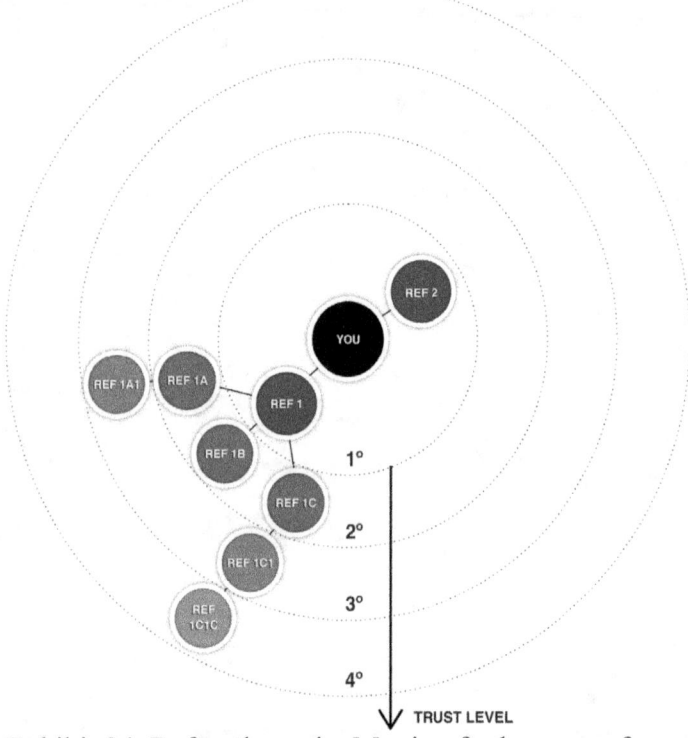

Exhibit 24. Referral matrix. Moving farther away from your first degree contacts lowers your trust of the person. Usually going past level 2 is the same as talking to a stranger.

There are a few freelance directory websites available these days that have contractors from all over the world on them. The two most popular are Elance.com and oDesk.com. Both of these allow you to filter results by country, level of experience, cost, reviews, etc.

Filter By:

Categories ⊖

☑ **All categories**

☐ Web Development (7,571)

☐ Software Development (4,267)

☐ Networking & Information Systems (1,514)

☐ Writing & Translation (1,437)

☐ Administrative Support (1,826)

☐ Design & Multimedia (2,845)

☐ Customer Service (688)

☐ Sales & Marketing (2,199)

☐ Business Services (577)

Feedback Score ⊖

☐ **Any Score**

☐ No Feedback Yet (680)

☑ 4.5 - 5.0 Stars (7,402)

☑ 4.0 - 4.5 Stars (1,399)

☐ 3.0 - 3.9 Stars (814)

☐ 2.0 - 2.9 Stars (218)

☐ 1.0 - 1.9 Stars (99)

Hourly Rate ⊖

$ per hour: Min - Max

Min   10   20   30   50   Max

Minimum Hours Billed ⊖

☐ **Any Hours**

☐ 1 hour or $1 earned (13,601)

☑ 100+ Hours (8,801)

☐ 1000+ Hours (3,077)

☐ Within Last 6 Months only (4,992)

Exhibit 25. Partial list of Odesk.com filters.

I don't recommend using these sites as your first line of research for a few reasons:
- You may not know exactly what you are looking for, so the search filters are not that meaningful.
- Several teams on these sites list skills that are highly questionable.
- The best folks with the most positive reviews are usually too busy and won't take on new work.
- Communication is slow and somewhat inefficient. Some of the American developers have day jobs and will only reply late at night, and the overseas developers work on different hours.

If you are a more seasoned project manager or know a good deal about technology, these sites can be good resources. But for a novice, I think they can actually do more harm than good.

The methods that tend to be a bit more productive in terms of choosing a developer revolve around finding verified experts.

I have had good success finding developers or tech teams via Amazon. The guys and gals who are smart enough to write a book and get positive reviews there usually run shops that are well structured and professional. The biggest benefit is that they are at the forefront of their industry and will usually provide "clean code." For instance, if you wanted a WordPress website, I would simply type in "wordpress development" in Amazon's search field and see which books on the topic have the best reviews. The authors of those books may take on your project or give strong recommendations of developers they respect. You may pay a premium for a published engineer, but you usually save time and money going with an expert. To contact a published author you can usually go to their website for their contact information. Otherwise, in the book itself they may mention how to initiate projects with them.

Another way to find tech personnel that usually works quite well is to e-mail the webmaster of a site you admire to inquire about who built it. With larger sites like CNN.com, they usually have internal teams. If you find a local company that has an amazing site, they most likely used a development shop. Most website owners are quite open to helping. Just be honest in your request.

Exhibit 26. Sample engineer reference request letter.

To whom it may concern:

I recently came across your website and have been reading it regularly. Not only is the content great, but I think your website design is one of the best I have ever seen.

I am in the midst of creating a new website for our company, which does _____ in [city name]. I have been having a bit of trouble finding a strong web programmer and designer in my area. Would you be open to sharing the contact information for your web designer?

I appreciate your time in advance. Once again, great website!

If you are ever in [city name], please do come by our store.

Sincerely,

[Your name]
[Your title]
[Your e-mail or phone number]

You don't have to go overboard on the letter; keep it short and simple. Sending one follow-up is more than acceptable. Also, if the website has a business phone number on it, feel free to call. Usually, you can get a web developer recommendation as well as other information, such as how the developer was to work with. Calling, in my experience, is more effective than an e-mail.

What should I be searching for?
Not coming from the tech industry, you may often feel lost when starting your search for a tech helper. Don't worry, everyone goes through this! There are way too many acronyms in the tech world. Even people in the industry can't keep up with them half of the time.

Let's say you want a website for your company. Since a website usually has many components, you want to keep your search rather broad so you can find a person that can help you on many fronts.

The most common way to refer to people who develop websites are the following:
- Web developer
- Website designer
- Web agency

Each of these searches may result in people with very different skill sets. Sometimes developers won't design and some designers won't code. The agency route tends to be the safest in terms of getting everything done, but it can be more expensive.

What should I ask?
When interviewing a web development firm, you really want to see how well-rounded their services are. You also want to make sure their services line up with your project goals.

For a business website, your basic goals are the following:
- It's easy to find.

- It's easy to update.
- It looks and feels like your brand image.

Simple questions to ask a web firm are the following:

- Can you make a site that I can update? Usually, they will answer yes. Ask them for a demo of a site they've built. Some companies may also offer you a "sandbox" site to play with to see if you like it. Consider this a free test drive. Any competent web firm can set up a sandbox site for you in less than an hour.
- What services do you offer for getting my site listed correctly in Google? Most companies will say they can do "SEO optimization." If a person codes according to current standards, the site has the foundation for search engine optimization or SEO. SEO itself is an ongoing process that cannot be done in one day. If the firm doesn't have a process for you to follow long-term, there is a good chance they are not SEO experts. The other thing about SEO optimization is that it requires a baseline to optimize from; you cannot start off being fully optimized. Be careful with people throwing around jargon.
- What services do you offer in terms of creative development? Do you write copy also? Some web firms may actually use templates when creating your site. There is nothing wrong with this, but make sure this is reflected in the price. If they do a custom design, it will obviously take a bit longer and potentially cost more.

These are basic questions about what the firm can offer. The downside is that you may not understand the answers, which is OK. What you should be concerned about is if the firm can take care of the whole project for you or if you will have to find multiple people to complete the project.

There are some operational questions that I also recommend asking:

Reference Checks:
Checking references for any person or firm is very important. I always ask to speak to at least three professional references. Most of the time references will give you overly positive reviews of how the relationship was. To read through the fluff, you as a potential employer should be looking for consistency amongst the three references. Did all the references have similar remarks about the communication skills or technical skill level? If you hear consistent themes come up you know the service provider or person is genuinely strong.

Team and communication
- Will I be dealing with one person on your team? How long has this person been with your team?
- What are your hours of operation?
- What time zone are you in?

- Do you outsource any of the work? If so, what part and why?
- Are you available to meet in person, Skype, or phone?
- How involved will I need to be?

Organization

- What project management tools do you use? Will I as the client have access to these tools during the project?
- Will we have a shared folder or place that we can swap documents or notes?
- Do you provide weekly updates?

Pricing

- What timekeeping system do you use?
- How do you charge for bug fixes?
- How are your milestone payments schedules created?
- What happens if you take more time on a job than you projected?
- Do you charge monthly maintenance fees after the project is finished?

Other

- If Google changes something that will affect our work together, will you inform me?
- Do you provide any stats or metrics for the sites you build?
- What are your expectations of the client in terms of time, communication, and technical expertise?
- Do you offer training in the systems that you are building?
- Do you recommend books I should read?
- Are you open to bartering for a portion of the fees?
- What is your process about getting requirements of features for the site down? The requirements are rules around how a particular feature should work and what technical resources it may need.
- What is your QA process?

For the most part, the majority of these questions should be answered in the RFP process.

How to set a budget

Usually, when sending out an RFP, you will get a wide range of price quotes back. Some of the firms may be overseas, some may underestimate costs, some assume that you will negotiate. The unfortunate truth is that there is no standard in terms of how web projects are priced.

The RFP process will give you an idea of where you will most likely end up in terms of pricing, but it is also good to have a budget in mind.

Most people undervalue their online presence, mainly because they are not sure what it will deliver in terms of revenue or customers. My suggestion here is to be open to various quotes.

For example, a small business in San Francisco wanted to update its website and add an online learning component to it. The business owner had no idea what to expect. She received proposals from $1,200 to $25,000. The low proposal was honest and said the bidding firm could not do the advanced online learning component but could get the basic website done within a few weeks. The firm that proposed the $25K accurately quoted the project but was well over the budget of the business owner.

In the end, the business owner went with the lower-priced proposal, not because it was cheaper, but because it was faster and took care of the immediate need, which was to refresh the look and feel of the site. The business owner decided she could wait for the online learning portion, since she was not sure she had time to manage it.

The lesson is that when it comes to deciding what you will actually pay for, you need to think about your original goals and if you can definitively drive a return on those goals in the short term.

Summary

Look for "verified" experts first. When choosing a team, ask them questions up front to see if there is a mutual fit. There is no cost associated with asking questions! And be open to cutting features to get to the price you are looking for.

Chapter 14 - Working with Your Tech Team and Getting Results

Getting results through people is a skill that cannot be learned in the classroom.
—John Paul Getty

An RFP, or request for proposal, is a document that lays out what you are looking for from your developers or creative folks.

The RFP itself is a great exercise for you to organize your thoughts and identify what is important to you and the project itself. The RFP closely follows your business plan and/or current business goals. If your goals are pretty straightforward, this document should be very easy to write.

The benefits of making an RFP are several fold:

- If a developer or creative person doesn't take time to read the RFP or ask questions, you'll immediately know they are not detail-oriented and probably not a good fit.
- An RFP makes developers think about timing, cost, technology, etc. It typically creates a much more in-depth conversation about the product itself, which usually makes the project stronger.
- The RFP can actually help you reduce features and focus on a simple project. More often than not, people get a bit too ambitious with all the features they want and then realize it will cost too much or take too long.
- It forces you to think about a budget and a goal for when you want your technology to go live. Creating this short-term goal is vital.
- The document can be used with many vendors at once. The goal is to get many quotes or bids at the same time. You can then negotiate price or other aspects. This puts you back in control.
- The RFP allows you to shop the project around with other firms to get the best price and find a team that you really click with.

The RFP process can be broken out into a few simple steps:
- First, the requestor creates the RFP and sends it out to a few vendors.
- Once the quotes come back, the requestor asks a few follow-up questions and potentially negotiates.
- Both parties commit to the project and work starts.

Simple right? What could possibly go wrong?

Lots.

Before we begin going into what comprises an RFP, I want to make something very clear. If you skimp on details within the RFP and rush through it, you are going to get a bad quote, and most likely your project will have several up-charges, and delays.

Investing time here is incredibly important!

What goes into an RFP?

The main components of an RFP can be boiled down into a few buckets.

- Brand
- Product/service
- Goals of project
- Team
- Competitors
- Design style
- Technology
- Timeline
- Budget
- Process of RFP
- Scope of expectations or deliverables
- Known issues

Brand

The brand section of an RFP is dedicated to describing your brand. The main issue is that a developer or creative person who doesn't know your product doesn't know what you stand for. Clearly explaining this helps him or her formulate a strategy or proposal that is in line with your brand. One of the worst things you can do is end up with a brand image online that differs significantly from your offline brand.

If your site looks like your deli, great! Similar colors, fonts, and styles of communication should be used.

Things to emphasize in the brand section are:

- What your brand stands for, described in two or three sentences from the owner's point-of-view.
- What your customers like about you, described in three to four bullets, or what customers know you for.
- How you are different from competitors.
- What values you are trying to convey.
- Your logo and company colors, if any.

Overall, this section is quite short. Keeping it simple and succinct will help the developers and engineers. And most importantly, don't use cliché terms or buzzwords. Focus on simplicity. Once you get into buzzwords, everyone has a different interpretation and people often tend to gloss over those terms. Meaningless buzzwords diminish the value of your brand.

Product or service

In this section of the RFP, all you are doing is simply describing your product or service.

If you sell sandwiches at a deli, describe where you are located, what types of sandwiches you make, and if it is a restaurant or a take-out establishment.

Include pictures if you can. Pictures are very powerful for telling your story.

Also, highlight your price point in this section. Are you offering a high-end organic sandwich or an affordable lunch sandwich?

Focus on the following information for the developer or creative person:

- Your product or service.
- What your product or service is called.
- The main features of the product or service.
- How people can purchase it.

In this section, you want to be quite detailed. If you have a video, that would be even better. But pictures are usually much more powerful than just a written description.

The goal here is to ensure that the developer or designer has a clear understanding of what you sell.

Goals of project

You can determine the goal, or it can be determined in a collaborative fashion. A good development firm will help you decide what is needed and what is not needed. It is easy to get caught up in new technology, so always remind yourself of the primary objective and your budget if you do decide to go down the road of the collaborative approach.

Focus on creating a foundation. What is your primary objective? With a website or basic application, the goal is usually tied to your foundational elements, which were discussed in chapter 4, exhibit 11.

Any good technical project should provide consumers information on how to find you, how to contact you, and what your product is. It should also emphasize your brand.

If you feel that your site is pretty strong to start with and you are approaching this as a redesign or feature addition, simply describe the goals of the features you are adding. For instance, if you are adding a Google map on your website, the goal would be to provide directions for people to find you.

If you are launching something for the first time, the goal might be a bit more basic, for example, a web presence to reference on business cards or inform people about what you do. Simple information.

Team

This section is actually quite simple. You want to identify your employees and who will be the main point of contact. If it is you for almost every situation, that is totally fine. It is important to let the developer or creative person know this.

Some other things you may want to highlight are your available hours, the best way to get in contact with you, and what your technical skill level is. Remember it is OK to say you are a novice!

Competitors

The competitor's section is a way of getting free market insight. If your competitor has been online for a while, there is a strong likelihood that they have done some testing or changes already. Use what they've learned so you don't have to reinvent the wheel. Sometimes you can monitor a competitor website over time and watch how they change layouts, colors, fonts, text, buttons or other things. This usually indicates a company testing elements to increase conversion. But beware; some companies just have crazy owners that like to change things for no reason at all. So monitor changes, but be cautious about emulating unless you can say to yourself that the new feature is a lot more intuitive.

If your RFP is for something basic like a website, the developer or designer will want to see URLs of your competitors' websites. You don't have to send them a copy of their magazine or TV ad. Comparing apples to apples here is quite important, so focus on showing competitor examples that are pertinent to your current project.

Now, there is one caveat to this rule. If for some reason you really like the design of a website that is not in your industry, you can reference it in the design section, which comes next.

Design

Most people don't have a design background; we only know what we like.

Professional web designers help us navigate the intricacies, and beauty, of the Internet. While there should be constructive communication, don't forget why you hired a designer in the first place: this is his or her area of expertise.

As a client, do you have the ability to make changes? Yes! By all means, if you don't like the design work, provide very specific comments about what you don't like and what elements you think you can keep. Work together to refine, but give the designer the freedom to do his or her job.

The best way of going about design projects is to get one mock-up in three different styles. Never have a designer build out everything and then start making changes. This is a waste of time and money. Building one page and coming up with a set of design rules will help the process move much quicker and faster.

The design section should include information about the following elements:

- Colors that you like or that your company is identified with.
- Any fonts that may be specific to your brand (most people don't have this, which is OK).
- Some guidelines around who makes up your audience. If your audience is older, you may want to design things to be a bit bigger.
- Information on how people usually interact with you. Will it be by smartphone or traditional computer? This will help the designer create a design that can scale based on the screen size.
- Will you need letterhead?
- Will you need a new logo?
- Do you need the design to be accessible by ADA standards?
- Will you need custom photographs?
- Will you need custom video?
- Information about the technology you are using. Usually the developer will talk directly to the designer, but if for some reason they are not, you should be able to convey this information.

Technology

Uh-oh, the dreaded technology section. Right about now, you are thinking, "I have no idea what I am looking for, so how am I supposed to make requirements for this?"

That is 100 percent OK!

You run a business, and it is not your responsibility to stay on top of every technology out there.

If you don't know how to describe what technology is important to you, it is best to approach this section with research, questions, and goals.

Technology goals are things that matter to you personally and to your customers. These are not tech terms.

For instance, goals for my personal site would be that it's fast, secure, easy to navigate, easy to find, and accessible via a smartphone.

If I were your customer, I think those goals would align pretty closely with what I am trying to achieve on your site. I need information, I want it fast, I don't want to get a virus, and I want to get it on my phone.

If you have the benefit of being able to talk to your customers, simply ask them, "Have you seen my website? Is there anything that you would change? Would you consider that change a high priority?" If for some reason you don't feel comfortable asking your customers questions like this, you can set up a simple focus-group test on a site like Userlytics.com or with Google's Consumer Surveys. Google's product is a bit cheaper, but Userlytics.com enables you to capture video and audio, which can be immensely important. Both are strong products and relatively easy to use.

Be careful not to get caught up in adding technical features, like making your site "social" if you do not know what that means. Any good developer will be able to add that in later once you are ready for it. If Facebook or Twitter aren't creating value for you, you may not need to add those features right now.

The above goals are more customer-centric. Now, I want you to think about managing your website.

Who on your team is going to keep this website up to date or edit it in the future? Do you want the developer to do everything for you, or do you want to administer it?

If you want to administer it, I suggest mentioning that you want a way of updating X page or Y picture.

Most developers can either include training in the proposal or create an interface that is as easy to use as Microsoft Word.

If you are slightly more advanced or have some special considerations or regulations, please make sure you convey those to the development team in the RFP.

As an example, if your company collects e-mail addresses, you may need to show your privacy policy before a person submits his or her address. If you are selling something online, you may need a secure processing feature to interface with the bank.

When talking about banking or money-transferring, we are really talking about your website communicating with other systems. This is usually referred to as a "call." For instance, if your website has a Facebook "like" button or if you want to include your Yelp reviews, you will need to make a call to Facebook or Yelp. Your engineer will know what this means, but it is important to define where you are getting your website information form.

Another important topic to cover in your RFP is asking the developers what their policy is for testing the site before it goes live and how they fix errors. Even the best of programmers may make the occasional error. You don't have to worry about the error itself, you have to worry about how they are going to fix it and how much it might potentially cost you.

In terms of accessibility, it might be important to state that you want your website to be accessible by phone, tablet, desktop, laptop, etc. You don't have to put a lot of detail into this, just noting it is helpful.

If you are building something like a phone app, you will need to be very specific about which phones you are designing the app for.

The top areas to focus on within the technology section are the following:

- Your personal goals and customer goals.
- Information on regulations.
- Security needs.
- Links to external systems.
- Where your information is coming from.
- Administration and maintenance.
- Expectations around compatibility.
- Expectations around fixing things.

Timeline
The timeline section of your RFP is very short. Focus on two things: when you would like to start the project, and when you would like to reasonably have it finished by.

Being reasonable here is key. If you do not know how long it might take to finish the project, you can say, "We would like to have this ready for X date, since we are launching a new ad campaign and want the site to coordinate with the campaign."

Creating a timeline is like a wedding, in some regards. Attendees don't usually plan enough ahead and need suit or dress alterations just days before the wedding. The tailor has a schedule and may project out two weeks, which doesn't meet your deadline. What do you do? You have the choice of going to another tailor, wearing the outfits as is, or paying a premium to get it done faster.

The other option is to leave the end-date open and just compare the proposals you receive. Most qualified engineers will project fairly similar completion times.

If one proposal comes in at ten weeks and another at one week, I would question both of them to find out what the differences are. Believe it or not, sometimes going with the shorter time frame may be a mistake. A slightly longer time frame may indicate that the developer is considering the whole cycle to produce something, including assessment, coding, testing, and fixing bugs.

If you are just building a simple informational website with basic text and pictures, it takes on average four to six weeks. Can it be done faster? Yes. Can it take longer? Yes.

When looking at the timeline, you also have to consider how much time *you* personally have to reply to questions, review the work, meet with the developer, and make edits. If it takes you two days to reply to an e-mail, you have just pushed out the timeline two days. Remember you and your schedule are part of the process!

Budget
Talking about money is never easy, especially with technical and creative projects. When creating an RFP, it is important to set forth what you are capable of paying.

You may have heard this before, but some people actually want to buy a Rolls-Royce, even though they can't afford one!

What happens in that situation?

The Rolls-Royce dealer wastes his time and the customer wastes his or hers.

Be realistic about what you can afford and try not to waste other people's time by saying you are open to all bids.

It is perfectly fine to say you have $5,000 to spend, or $500 or $50,000. Creating a budget is important to make sure that things don't get out of hand. You can keep building forever online. The other part of this is that you want to think of your tech project as an investment. If you were to spend $50,000 on a project, would you be able to recoup that cost through additional sales? If not, you are putting money in the wrong place.

If, for some reason, you are unsure how much you will make from the project, that is OK. Lots of times it is hard to measure these things. You can always pick a different metric, like customer satisfaction. For instance, you may not drive sales on your website, but you may have customers tell you it was really easy to find your menu online with their phone.

Some developers may have a minimum to work with them, while others are quite flexible.

Many people are shocked by how much developers or creative folks can cost. Of course, this cost varies greatly by region. Check out the chart below as a reference point.

These figures are ranges only. Actual rates may be higher or lower based on skill level. These figures are based on 2012 estimates. My goal here is to give you a basic idea of how much decent talent costs.

Region	Developers	Creative
West	$90 to $150 an hour	$40 to $80 an hour
East	$90 to $120 an hour	$40 to $80 an hour
South	$70 to $110 an hour	$30 to $70 an hour
Central	$55 to $100 an hour	$20 to $65 an hour
Asia	$10 to $65 an hour	$10 to $30 an hour
Easter Europe	$20 to $40 an hour	NA
South America	$20 to $50 an hour	NA

Exhibit 26 – Sample hourly rates for developers and creative folks

If you're enticed by the rates outside the US, consider whether you'll be able to manage the team given the time differences and potential communication issues. My personal experience is that paying a premium to work with a local worker usually results in a faster turnaround and fewer communication issues. In several cases, I have used foreign developers and it turned out to be more expensive; they may charge you half the price, but then they bill three times as many hours. And on top of that, I needed a local person to debug the work. Your experience may differ, but if you do decide to use a foreign developer, make sure you have a strong project manager in place.

How should you approach your budget? Since the scope of your project may vary from your neighbor's technology needs, it is hard to provide a specific guideline for what you should be spending.

There are some powerful hints, though, that can help you limit the amount of money you'll need to spend up front:

- Ask for a payment plan. *Never ever* pay for the whole project up front. If a developer asks you for that, walk away quickly. A payment plan usually requires a 10 to 20 percent deposit up front and then payments based upon completion of certain milestones. The last milestone should be based upon your formal final approval. If you are not happy with something, or something is broken, make sure you hold payment until it is fixed.
- Barter. If you are a mom-and-pop business selling pizza, most developers or engineers may be open to trading food for a portion of the payment. If you find someone willing to take just food for payment, they may have a low experience level. Stronger developers will have a steady flow of work that will make the barter seem less attractive, but most people are somewhat flexible.
- Use credit cards. Most developers or creative folks will accept some form of electronic payment like PayPal. Most tech and creative shops these days do not take credit cards due to the fees. However, your credit card may have a significant rewards or cash-back program, so it never hurts to ask. By using a credit card, you also get another fifteen to thirty days to pay off the balance, helping your cash flow.

- Negotiate! Even though a developer may quote a rate of $100 an hour, once he or she scopes out the whole project, most are willing to work with a client to get things within a budget. For instance, if the project estimate is one hundred hours, which works out to $10,000, but your budget is $8,000, your developer may come down a bit, but you may also have to come up a bit. The other option is to go back through the scope of work and remove features.

Coming up with a budget is a process of sorts; it may continue to change and evolve. The key thing is don't spend more than you have. I would say never skimp on the quality of a developer; focus instead on reducing features. You can always add on to a strong, well-built platform. It takes way more money to fix and rebuild a sub-par platform. Always focus on quality. It pays off long-term.

The RFP process
When putting your RFP together, you really want to be very clear with potential vendors how you will make your decision.

Things to include in this section are details about the following:
- The deadline for submitting the proposal.
- When you will ask clarifying questions.
- When you plan on making a formal decision or choosing a vendor.
- Whether you will have a short list of vendors.

Overall, this section is very brief. It helps vendors plan their schedules accordingly and know when they should follow up with you.

Scope of expectations
In this section, the goal is to clearly tell the vendor what you expect to see in the formal proposal. The vendor *must* address these topics to be considered.

The things I consider important to understanding more about a vendor or developer are the following:

- A proposed project plan with details about tools. Strong developers will use project management tools that allow you to see what is going on at all times. If they don't have a way you can monitor their work, do not pay by the hour. You have no way of proving how much time they spent on the project. The advantages of the online project management tools are that they are collaborative and allow you to have a running history of questions, answers, issues, etc. This becomes very valuable after the project is finished. The project plan will also show major milestones.
- Cost breakdown that coordinates to the project plan. The project plan might show that the engineer works fifty hours and the creative person twenty hours. If those people have different rates, they should be shown

as different line items. You may also need licenses, hardware, stock photos, etc. All of that should be broken out in the cost estimate.

- Examples of past projects. These should be somewhat relevant to your project in terms of scope. Ask the vendors for details like how long the projects took and the costs involved.
- References. References are incredibly important. Later on in the book, I will have a section about what to ask a reference to get a less biased view. References should include a person's name, e-mail, and phone information. Usually, I request at least three references and talk to a minimum of two. If the vendor can't provide three references, use this to negotiate your price.
- Policies regarding fixes. It is good to know what a developer's policy is for fixing bugs and what he or she considers a bug. Most developers won't charge to fix a bug, but some may charge for a bug if it happens after your formal sign-off. This is an area for negotiation!
- Pricing for long-term maintenance. After the initial build-out, many vendors will offer you a discounted rate for monthly maintenance or updates. For example, if the original rate is $100 per hour, the vendor may charge $85 per hour for monthly updates if he or she can sell you five hours a month. It works out to be a retainer, in some regards. Don't feel forced to buy this right away. You can always add it on later. Another thing to consider is if you plan on using a developer twenty to thirty hours a month, it might be cheaper in some cases to hire an in-house person.
- Questions about the project. Vendors who have read your whole RFP will have questions to clarify things. If they don't, there is a high chance they didn't read the whole RFP or skimmed over it. Getting questions out of the way in the beginning is important to keeping cost overruns low and staying on schedule. Make this a required portion of the proposal. They may ask questions prior to submitting the proposal also.
- Justification of a specific technology or method. In certain cases, you may have asked for the site to be built using X technology and the developer recommends Y technology. You want to make sure the vendor justifies that decision and provides specific examples of why it is a better option or a potential cost savings. If the vendor just says, "That is what I know best," you can either move on or push him or her to justify it. Remember, you are the customer, and you are the one who has to live with this site for a while. Being comfortable with the technology is important.
- Information about the team. A strong vendor will tell you who is on the team and where they are located, make references to their blogs, and mention their certifications.

Known issues

This section in the RFP usually talks about some things you know are important to your business, like certain government regulations, if you need your site to be accessible for handicapped individuals, etc. All of this information is important for the vendor when he or she is putting together the quote.

How to decide on a quote

As you can see, the RFP process is not quick. Just writing the RFP may take you a few hours. But spending that time up front will save you time later on.

It will usually take about two weeks to get qualified quotes back from various vendors. Once you get the quotes, the next step is figuring out which quote you want to go with.

Start with broad strokes.

Figure out which proposals come close to your budget. If a proposal is two or three times your budget, don't immediately take it out of the running. Simply ask the vendor why the quote was so much higher than their competitors'. Often, there is a misunderstanding of a key feature. Other times, the vendor is just not a good fit.

Next, look at who delivered exactly what you asked for in the deliverables. If a vendor missed a significant section, this is usually a red flag; the vendor is just not detail-oriented.

Once you narrow the field a bit, it is time to focus on calling references.

When speaking to references, there are a few key questions to ask:
- Did the vendor meet the deadline?
- What was the vendor's communication level during the project? Were there any times you felt in the dark or that the vendor was arrogant?
- Have you worked with other developers or designers? If so, how would this vendor's team rank or compare?
- Was the vendor accessible after the project was finished?
- Did you find any major errors in the work?
- Would you recommend the vendor, or do you have another developer you can refer me to?

Most references come back pretty positive. That is a big problem. It is really hard to know if they are telling the truth. For each positive reference, how many negative experiences were there?

The one thing I have noticed with references is that the ones that come through as tepid are usually indicators of a so-so vendor. If all three come back extremely consistent and really emphatic, then that usually indicates a strong vendor, one who has gone above and beyond to deliver a high-quality product.

People who deliver OK quality get OK reviews. You can essentially ask a reference any question you want and listen to how enthusiastic the person is about the response. The main thing to look for is consistently high enthusiasm. When you hear consistency in the remarks, you know the quality of service was very high.

Evaluating a quote is a somewhat tedious process. But think of it this way: the time you are spending here is not costing you anything. Properly vetting a vendor helps you save money by investing in the right person. Making a quick decision without checking references could result in a major financial loss.

How to spot a scammer
Scammers are relatively easy to spot.

Key indicators of a scammer are the following:

- When you ask the vendor where the team is, he or she gives you vague answers. Most of the time this means the vendor is just outsourcing to another team.
- The vendor says yes to everything.
- The timeline or price is significantly shorter or cheaper than any other quote. Sometimes vendors bid very low to get you interested and then hit you with a series of add-ons and up-charges.
- The vendor doesn't have any references.
- The vendor doesn't want to meet you in person or Skype with you. Seeing a person's face is an amazing trust-builder.
- The vendor responds to e-mails only late at night. Usually this means he or she is in a different time zone on the other side of the planet or has another job.
- The vendor won't get on the phone. This usually indicates poor communication skills.
- There are spelling errors in the vendor's e-mails.
- The vendor misses the first milestone. This usually indicates he or she will miss many more.
- The vendor sends you a bunch of sites as references, but no people to talk to. In the past, I have seen developers or designers use other people's work as their own.

How should you work with your vendor?

In my experience, the best working relationships are built around knowing what each team member can do. If you try to force the designer to make the site look a certain way or you try to manage every tiny detail of the project, you will end up frustrating the team members and usually creating a product that is somewhat "Frankenstein-ed." What I mean is that the project is just a mix of random parts, nothing matches and things don't work very smoothly. It is usually a direct result of groupthink. Too many cooks in the kitchen can really ruin the final project.

Exhibit 27. Frankenstein's monster. A random mix of parts that didn't go so well…
http://upload.wikimedia.org/wikipedia/commons/thumb/a/a7/Frankenstein's_monster_(Boris_Karloff).jpg/300px-Frankenstein's_monster_(Boris_Karloff).jpg

To define who is on your team and each member's skill set, simply write down a team description and assign roles.

Here is an example:

Joe is the storeowner and person requesting the project. He will be responsible for milestone sign-off and providing key creative assets, like logos or copy.

Charlie is the head engineer who will be responsible for creating user flows, the database, server set-up, and bug fixes. Charlie will directly coordinate with the designer.

Laura is the designer and will be responsible for coming up with the look and feel of the site and providing direction to the engineer for things like navigation, copy, and usability. Laura will also act as the project manager, communicating directly with the client about milestone updates and various questions.

The above role definition helps accomplish a few things. Joe can now e-mail Laura directly with questions and know that she will relay information to Charlie, if necessary. It also shows that Joe will be active in the review process. Lastly, it establishes Laura as the design expert, giving her a bit more decision-making authority.

Pay attention to this.

One of the most important things you can do with the organizational chart is to make sure everyone on the team reads it and acknowledges it. If you keep it to yourself then there is greater potential for miscommunication.

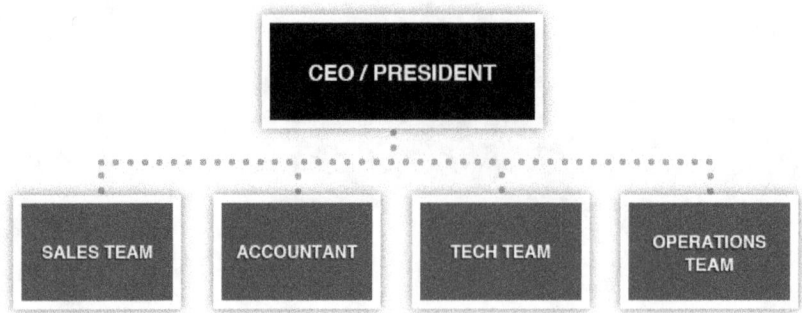

Exhibit 28. Sample organizational chart.

How to test in the QA process

Owning a small business, it's easy to think that everyone who puts his or her name behind a product will deliver a quality product. Unfortunately, this is not the case. I have run into several technology firms that are more focused on churning through a project rather than getting it 100 percent right. The main reason is that it is almost impossible to get things 100 percent right.

What are quality assurance tests? Most of the time, you are testing common user scenarios. For instance, if a person comes to your website and wants to search for your location, does the search box work? Does the navigation work? Is the map page accurate and easy to read? Does the map page look consistent on a PC versus a Mac? Is it usable on a mobile device?

This is something I want all small business owners to realize: with technology, there is a certain amount of error that is inherent in each project. It is like if you were to make 100,000 plastic bottles—a certain percentage will have minor defects.

You're probably thinking, "Why am I paying for shoddy work?" People never pay for shoddy work in the technology world. They pay for bad processes.

How can you avoid being part of a bad process?

There are two main ways of doing this.

You can either build quality into the process itself by having regular quality assurance checks along the way, or you can do extensive quality assurance checking at the end of the process.

There are pros and cons to each.

Doing QA during the process itself may slow down the entire project. If you stop to fix each error, everything dependent on that feature will be pushed back. Most developers do not build timelines around this process. The focus is usually getting things out the door as fast as possible, which doesn't leave much room for fixing and tweaking.

Given that most engineers and creative folks do not use this type of quality assurance checking, I recommend against forcing it upon them. Even though people like the concept of building quality into the system, they don't like waiting for it.

The second option is to do quality assurance tests at the end.

To effectively check for errors in a technology product, you really have to approach it as a regular user and go through every feature on the site.

When you find something that doesn't work at all or doesn't work as expected, the process is to mark it as a bug for the team to fix.

The third part of the QA process is to verify that the bug has been fixed properly. If it has been fixed or resolved, the bug is considered closed.

Sometimes, with major bugs, the team may have to decide if the time required to fix it is worth delaying the product itself. The quickest way to decide this is to ask, "Does this prevent a user from achieving one of the main uses of our site?" If the answer is yes, fix the bug and delay the release. If the answer is no, don't worry, you can fix things in the background and update the site later on.

This is a quick and dirty version of how to do QA. If you are working on a larger project, make sure all the use cases are documented and the results of each case are also documented somewhere. It may be a pain to document, but it will be worthwhile, especially if you have frequent turnover on your team or several parties touching the site at once.

Pay attention to the proposal that your engineer or creative person delivers to you! Make sure it includes a reasonable amount of time for QA.

QA process simplified:
- Write down use cases of the site.
- Test the site against these uses cases, marking issues as bugs.
- Fix bugs.
- Verify that bugs are fixed.

Exhibit 29. Sample use cases for QA testing.

Sample Use Case 1. Searching for directions with main navigation.
Intended outcome is that the user should be able to find the "directions" button and should end up on a map page.

If the user cannot find the button, that is one potential issue. If the user hits the button and nothing happens, that is a bug.

Sample Use Case 2. User wants to see a menu online.
Intended outcome is that the user should be able to find "menu" on the navigation and load the page.

As with the previous use case, there is always the issue that the person cannot find the navigation button. However, that is not a bug, it is more of a design issue.

With something like a menu, it might be stored as a picture, PDF, or regular text. If the user is on a mobile phone and the page does not load correctly, that is a bug. If the photo does not show up, that is a bug.

When testing, it is important to take note of how you were testing the use case, what device you were using, and what error you saw. If you don't record these pieces of information, it is very hard to replicate the error and fix it. Engineers rely greatly on the ability to replicate an error.

If you do not provide use cases or parameters around what is being tested, the person doing QA can end up doing too many unstructured tasks, which takes a long time. A set number of tasks is key to making the QA process fast and focused.

How to set aside features for version 2.0

With a technology project, there is an inevitable deadline, which is usually called the "go-live date." On this day, the public should be able to access your product.

There are a few common issues with project management in small businesses.

First, teams pick the deadline arbitrarily. They just say on December 1, we are going to turn it on. That might be five days away and completely unrealistic from a development standpoint. Depending on a reasonable estimate from your development team is key to arranging your deadline. For instance, let's say today's date is September 1. The project you would like to release will take six weeks of work. Your team observes Jewish holidays, and you are personally traveling three weeks during this period.

At first glance, your deadline might be October 15 or so. But given the holidays and your travel schedule, you may want to accommodate for a slightly more realistic timeline.

With your team, you may say, "Let's finish the project by October 15." However, from a personal expectation level, you may be fine for the project to go live on November 1 and still be considered a success.

Deadlines are vital in the RFP and development process. Accommodating for holidays, travel, QA, and unforeseen issues is the sign of an experienced project manager.

One of the hardest things a business owner may have to do is tell the team they need to remove a feature to meet the deadline. With some projects, the deadline is more important than the product itself, since there are other factors present like intense competition.

If you need October 15 as your go-live date, you may need to remove a feature from the project. I suggest removing features that are nonessential to the customer.

For example, if you had planned to add a really cool game to the site but it is not related to your core user goals, remove it and push it into version two of the site.

Version two of a product is really comprised of two main components: any and all features that didn't make it into version one and features customers provided feedback on. How do you know what features your customer is looking for? Simple, check your Contact Us e-mail! Customers are very vocal these days and will often tell you if something is broken or "You know, it would be great if you had X." The other option, which costs nothing, is to just ask the customers who come in. Did they find what they needed easily and quickly on the website? What did they have problems with? Take notes and label them as *Customer Wants and Needs for Version Two.*

Surprisingly, I wouldn't recommend that you add new features from your pipeline in version two. The reason is that if you focus on what your customer is saying, you become a more responsive organization and more customer-focused. This is better than being focused on just creating new features that are untested, unfounded, and may not drive any revenue. Start out by focusing on revising existing content rather than adding new features.

Summary
Creating a product really needs a lot stamina and some compromise. Deadlines are very important to help get things out the door, but realize you may have to cut features to get everything done on time or cost. When creating a new version or updating your website, it is very important to get feedback directly from your customers. Don't make assumptions!

Chapter 15 - Who Is on Your Team?

Individual commitment to a group effort - that is what makes a team work, a company work, a society work, a civilization work. - Vince Lombardi, Legendary Coach

Drawing from experience, one of the biggest issues I ran into was that small businesses didn't define who would be doing what during the project. This usually caused confusion but more importantly it didn't designate one person as the project owner. If there is no owner the project was rarely completed. The tricky thing with small business is that there may only be one or two people in the company. In cases like this it becomes a bit more important to first figure out how you can make time for a new project and establishing a goal. If you can't make time or a goal, the project itself is somewhat doomed.

As you already know, every small business owner wears every hat imaginable: accountant, marketer, janitor, etc.

But how often do you, as the owner, take the time to formally define what each person or role within your company is supposed to do?

The point of this exercise is not to create more overhead for your business but to actually help you hire people quickly when you need them.

The other benefits of this exercise are the following:
- Documenting who is responsible for what task at the moment. This helps eliminate overlap of people doing the same task and ignoring other key tasks.
- Creating an organizational chart. Once you know what the roles are in your business, you can arrange them to ensure proper reporting structure.
- Skill set evaluation. For instance, a lot of business owners have to take care of accounting but have never had any formal training in it. From the 30,000-foot viewpoint, this is a good way to prioritize who you want to hire first.

Defining team members

Here are a few convenient steps to understand more about your team. This worksheet should be filled out for each business role. These worksheets end up being your job descriptions, which can be easily copied into a job posting.

Worksheet describing each role:

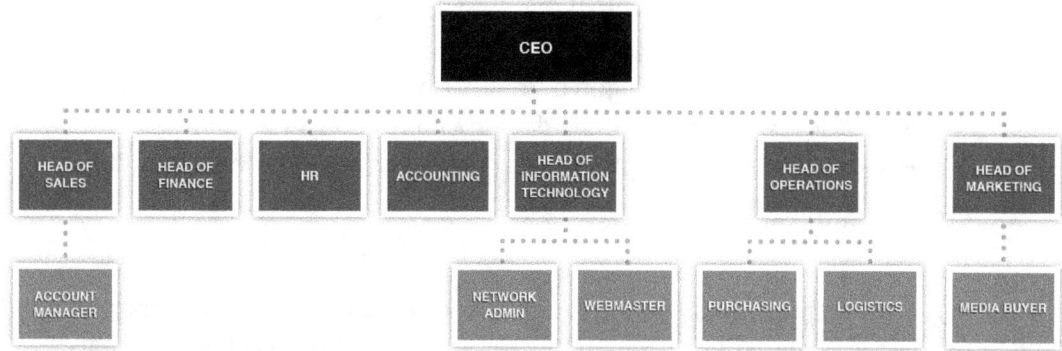

Exhibit 30. Sample organizational structure.

Role - This is an informal title of what you call this person internally. The other thing that a role can mean within a small company is that each person may wear multiple hats. For instance, at the deli, the founder may handle all accounting and cooking of food. He or she has two roles but one title.

Title - If you have an official title for the role, place it here. This is helpful when hiring, since other people tend to identify with common titles, which results in more applicants.

Reports to - Whom does this person report to? If you currently have a one-person team, don't feel obligated to have everyone report to you. You can add in middle management as a long-term buffer.

Manages - Whom does this person manage, if anyone? Is there a team of people supervised by the person in this role?

Responsibilities. What is this person responsible for? For instance, in the example of the accountant, he or she would be responsible for all incoming monies, paying partners/vendors, paying rent, managing travel expense reports, and coming up with weekly balance sheets.

Requirements - Given the responsibilities above, what tools or skills does this person need to complete the work successfully? Some things to consider:

- Physical capabilities - For example, FedEx requires that an employee is able to lift fifty pounds.
- Technical knowledge - What software or devices does this person need to know how to use?
- Education - Is a particular education or certification necessary for the job? For many positions, you don't really need a college degree. Think about how this might impact the salary you pay this person. If you don't need a person with a college degree, why pay for one?

- Language capabilities - Will this person be using any other languages to communicate during the day?
- Location - Where is this job currently done?
- Schedule - What hours of the day do you need this person in the office? Are the hours related to the work, or can the work be done anytime during the day?

Summary

Knowing who is on your team and what role each person plays is key to understanding who will create goals, who will be accountable for goals, and how to make the goals happen.

With small businesses, completing this worksheet might seem like a time-intensive task, but it can help air a lot of frustrations within a small team.

Another benefit is that you start to identify gaps in your team which may help with future hiring needs.

Chapter 16 - Finding the right Talent

The key for us, number one, has always been hiring very smart people.
—Bill Gates

Defining the roles in your company can be an eye-opening experience. But one of the hardest tasks associated with it is delegating these roles. To effectively delegate, you might have to bite the bullet and hire some new staff. Here is a quick guide to hiring people who can do the heavy lifting for your technology needs.

It is often very hard to hire for technology positions for several reasons:

- You have never done the job yourself, so you are not sure what skills are needed.
- The technology is so new, you are not even sure what to ask and many people just say they know it.
- You have no way of measuring success.
- Cutting-edge tech is usually expensive, making the risk even greater.
- You have no process for managing this person.
- You have no goals for the process since it is foreign.

When interviewing small businesses, I've found that there are essentially two groups of business owners when it comes to technology: the do-it-yourself crowd and the hire-anyone crowd.

Both these strategies can be detrimental to your business. Doing it yourself will help you learn the tech, but do you really have the time? Will your core business suffer if you were to step away for three to five days straight?

Hiring with a shotgun approach usually results in low-quality talent and no real results. Sometimes you get lucky and hire a gem of a worker, but this is usually less than 1 percent of the time.

Let's focus on increasing your odds of success.

In previous chapters, we covered how to create a management hierarchy and full job descriptions.

Now we have the challenge of interviewing people on topics we ourselves are not familiar with.

Let's break this down into a process so it can easily be replicated. For the purpose of this section, let's assume you already posted the job and now have a few resumes to review.

The sample job descriptions below are templates you can use to help you find potential web developers, an app developer, or a social media manager. Replace the words in brackets with your own information. Even though these are templates to get you started, please feel free to edit them, add your own flair, and change the requirements. Each job description is set up to be fairly general, which should get you a wide swath of resumes or proposals.

If you want the person to only work with you on one project, make sure to highlight that it is a project, not a full-time job.

Sample job description for a web developer
[Company name] is a company based in [city name] that sells [product or service name].

Our current project is to [project title with description]. It requires a person that has a broad set of skills in web development.

Our minimum requirements for this job are:
- Fluency in HTML5 and CSS3.
- Knowledge of major content management systems and the ability to talk about pros and cons of each.
- Experience with QA and debugging.
- Knowledge of front-end and back-end technologies
- Ability to architect and create databases.
- Knowledge of current security protocols.
- Knowledge of APIs for major payment gateways and/or maps.
- Ability to build a site that is responsive to a variety of devices and operating systems.
- Strong written and oral communication skills
- Strong references from previous projects.
- You must be located in [country name] and available during the hours of 9:00 a.m. to 5:00 p.m. [time zone].
- Knowledge of current W3C or ADA accessibility guidelines.
- Ability to work with deadlines and goals.
- Excellent organizational skills.

The project entails building a website from scratch. Our main goal is to [how it will help customers].

Our technical skill level is [novice, mid-level, expert]. We are looking for a web developer who will complement our team and help it grow in a sustainable manner.

Your core tasks will be to:
- Gather requirements from our team members and potentially customers.

- Come up with an architecture that is sustainable, easily maintained, and cost effective.
- Prioritize tasks or features to ensure timely delivery. This will entail working with several stakeholders.
- Test the site before it goes live to ensure there are no bugs.
- Provide ongoing site maintenance or teach our staff how to maintain the site.
- Inform our team of the most relevant new technologies for our business. We are not looking to know every new technology, but we are interested in technologies that can drive new customers and more revenue or reduce costs.

We are open to proposals around technologies to use. We are looking for a [long-term/short-term] relationship.

What we are offering:
- A great work environment that has [unique characteristics about your business].
- Benefits - [like health insurance, free food, or free coffee]

How to apply:
- Include a copy of your most recent resume or CV in PDF format.
- Include a cover letter that highlights why you would like to work with us and what makes you amazing.
- List of three references with phone numbers and e-mail addresses.
- List of three reference projects with a description of your role in each project.
- Send all the information above to [yourname@yourcompany.com or your postal mailing address] by [deadline date].
- When applying via e-mail, please include the title of the job and your name in the subject line.

Not following the directions above will immediately disqualify your application.

[Company name] is an equal opportunity employer. Applicant must be a [country] citizen or have a current and valid work visa.

Sample job description for an app developer
[Company name] is a company based in [city name] that sells [product or service name].

Our current project is to [app project title and detailed application description/business model]. It requires a person who has a broad set of skills in app development.

Our minimum requirements for this job are:
- Fluency in HTML5 and CSS3.

- Knowledge of [Android, iOS, Blackberry, Windows Mobile] platforms and app store requirements.
- Knowledge of tablet and smartphone app development.
- Knowledge of major content management systems and the ability to talk about pros and cons of each.
- Experience with QA and debugging.
- Knowledge of front-end and back-end technologies.
- Ability to architect and create databases.
- Knowledge of current security protocols.
- Knowledge of APIs for major payment gateways, maps, and [Facebook, Twitter, Google+].
- Ability to build a site that is responsive to a variety of devices and operating systems.
- Strong written and oral communication skills.
- Strong references from previous projects.
- Location in [country name] and availability during the hours of 9:00 a.m. to 5:00 p.m. [time zone].
- Knowledge of current W3C or ADA accessibility guidelines.
- Ability to work with deadlines and goals.
- Excellent organizational skills.
- Excellent UX interface design skills.
- Knowledge of A/B testing methodologies.

The project entails building an app from scratch. Our main goal is to [how you'd like the app to help customers].

Our technical skill level is [novice, mid-level, expert]. We are looking for an app developer who will complement our team and help it grow in a sustainable manner.

Your core tasks will be to:
- Gather requirements from our team members and potential customers.
- Come up with an architecture that is sustainable, easily maintained, and cost-effective.
- Prioritize tasks or features to ensure timely delivery. This will entail working with several stakeholders.
- Test the site before it goes live to ensure there are no bugs.
- Provide ongoing site maintenance or teach our staff how to maintain the site.
- Inform our team of the most relevant new technologies for our business. We are not looking to know every new technology, but we are interested in technologies that can drive new customers and more revenue or reduce costs.

We are open to proposals around technologies to use. We are looking for a [long-term/short-term] relationship.

What we are offering:
- A great work environment that has [unique characteristics about your business].
- Benefits - [like health insurance, free food, or free coffee].

How to apply:
- Include a copy of your most recent resume or CV in PDF format.
- Include a cover letter that highlights why you would like to work with us and what makes you amazing.
- List of three references with phone numbers and e-mail addresses.
- List of three reference projects with a description of your role in each project.
- Send all the information above to [yourname@yourcompany.com or your postal mailing address] by [deadline date].
- When applying via e-mail, please include the title of the job and your name in the subject line.

Not following the directions above will immediately disqualify your application.

[Company name] is an equal opportunity employer. Applicant must be a [country] citizen or have a current and valid work visa.

Sample job description for a social media analyst or manager
[Company name] is a company based in [city name] that sells [product or service name].

Our current project is to get our business up and running on major social media outlets like, Facebook, Google+, and Twitter. It requires a person with a broad set of social media skills and a deep understanding of how the various social networks work.

Our minimum requirements for this job are:
- Knowledge of basic HTML to create links and verify that social media traffic is trackable.
- Strong copywriting skills. Fluency in English is a must.
- Photography skills are a plus, but not essential.
- Deep understanding of how to post, share, gather followers, and engage in conversations on behalf of our company across social media platforms.
- Addiction to social media and use of the various networks from your desktop or mobile device daily.
- Strong organizational skills. Being deadline-oriented is important.
- Ability to work with goals and analytics. We will be looking for revenue growth or cost reductions through our social media efforts. Measuring this success will be key.

- Familiarity with Google Webmaster tools and/or Google Local tools.
- Proficiency with MS Office applications.

The project entails building a social presence from scratch. Currently, we have a website, but we wish to expand our reach on the social networks. We need an individual who can guide us and execute consistently.

Our technical skill level is [novice, mid-level, expert]. We are looking for a social media [analyst /manager] who will complement our team and help it grow in a sustainable manner. We would like to focus on creating a high-quality [product/service] and enable our customers to build our reputation for us.

Your core tasks will be to:
- Create a social media strategy.
- Create an according timeline with milestones or goals.
- Create metrics to measure the goals.
- Create relevant blog posts and/or social network posts on a regular schedule.
- Train our staff how social media works and how we can potentially integrate it into our daily lives.
- Provide briefs or updates to the whole team about how the social media push is working.

We are open to proposals around technologies to use. We are looking for a [long-term/short-term] relationship.

What we are offering:
- A great work environment that has [unique characteristics about your business].
- Benefits [like health insurance, free food, or free coffee].

How to apply:
- Include a copy of your most recent resume or CV in PDF format.
- Include a cover letter that highlights why you would like to work with us and what makes you amazing.
- List of three references with phone numbers and e-mail addresses.
- List of three reference projects with a description of your role in each project.
- Send all the information above to [yourname@yourcompany.com or your postal mailing address] by [deadline date].
- When applying via e-mail, please include the title of the job and your name in the subject line.

Not following the directions above will immediately disqualify your application.

[Company name] is an equal opportunity employer. Applicant must be a [country] citizen or have a current and valid work visa.

Now that resumes are pouring in, here is a seven-step process for what you do next.

How to effectively use the sample job descriptions

I encourage you to use these job descriptions verbatim or modify them as per your needs. The intent of these descriptions is to give you a head start with your recruiting. The job descriptions are set up rather broad and try to use current terminology but given that technology changes so rapidly, you may want to update them with your specific needs.

Using job descriptions like these in the past has netted a lot of resumes for me personally. I usually post them in at least two to three places, including the corporate website, Craigslist and a larger Internet job board. The quality of candidates you get from each website will differ and it will ultimately be up to you to filter through the resumes.

Given the broad nature of these job descriptions you may often find that people start listing out that they can do everything you listed. Make sure to ask them to provide examples or instances of when they worked with each technology. This helps ensure they are not over selling their talent.

Summary

Spending time defining exactly what you are looking for and how you want your organization perceived can really help you set the stage for a great corporate culture. Hiring haphazardly usually results in poor project outcomes or even higher costs.

Chapter 17 - How to hire
Time spent on hiring is time well spent. – Robert Half

Part 1
Reviewing resumes
When gathering resumes, you always have one of two problems: too many resumes or not enough.

If you don't have enough, you need to go back to the original job description and revise there. Do not make a decision on a new candidate if you only have two or three resumes.

For argument's sake, lets assume you have too many resumes. We need to rank the most important things for you and your business on a broad level. Start with broad cuts to get to a preliminary short list.

Let's get rid of the monkeys first.

- Include instructions in the original job posting. For example, tell candidates they must submit a resume, an original cover letter, and a link to the About Us section of your website. Most of the time, people send out tons of applications and don't follow directions correctly. Get rid of those people immediately. They are not detail-oriented. This one trick usually eliminates around 80 percent of applicants, if not more.
- Look for spelling or grammar errors. If you see any, throw away the resume. The person is not a strong communicator and is not detail-oriented. MS Word can be a great way to quickly review resumes. Just look for the red or green underlines that automatically spot the errors. That is usually the quickest way to find errors. Be careful with this, though; sometimes Word picks up people's names as an error.

Once you are done with the broad strokes, you'll usually end up with five to ten resumes. This number is actually quite manageable.

At this point, shifting to a more personal tactic is usually beneficial.

Part 2
Screening calls
Calling five to ten candidates can be somewhat time-consuming, but the fact is that you are hiring a person for the long-term, not for a one- to two-day job. Investing up front is always going to pay off in this process.

I usually limit screening calls to thirty minutes, and most run around fifteen minutes. I set them up early in the day to verify that the person is responsible in the morning and will show up on time to work. Feel free to set up calls starting at 8:00 a.m. If an applicant declines the call without a good reason, just move on; he or she is lazy. If a person really wants a job, they will do whatever it takes to work around you.

During the call, break it up into four parts:

- Explain what your company does. Take five minutes to briefly explain what you sell and how this role might fit into the big picture. Be very specific to communicate your enthusiasm for your product and the fact that several people replied to the job posting. You want to introduce a certain sense of urgency and competition. Do not go into buzzword terms or oversell your product/service.

  At this point, you may want to check with the candidate and ask if he or she understood what you were talking about. If you get a quick "Yes, I got all of that," ask the candidate to repeat it in his or her own words. If the candidate fumbles, don't worry. Keep moving along in the process.

- Question the candidate's resume. This is usually the hardest part. I find that most resume bullet points don't always relate to my own product or service. What you are really looking for are specific skills that can be leveraged in your company or skills that will allow you to teach the candidate your business.

  If you are looking for skills that indicate a person is willing to learn, try to aim for the following, which should help you create a picture of this person's critical thinking skills:
  — Communication skills - Keep this simple. If the candidate sounds enthusiastic and is communicating thoughts clearly, that is usually sufficient during a phone interview.
  — Organization skills - This one is a bit tougher to assess on the phone. A good indicator is to ask them how they would organize a giant bag of Legos. There is no right answer, but if they start to mention organizing by number of bumps, color, or shape, then they have the skills to learn a larger organizational system.
  — Analytical skills - Once again, this is somewhat hard to assess via phone. A simple way around this is to ask the candidate to come up with two or three metrics to measure the performance of a newspaper.
  — Eagerness - Assessing eagerness is a somewhat gut judgment. Usually, you can identify a potential winner by asking the candidate to tell you about a work situation where he or she was highly successful. Don't look for marginal success. If they didn't have great success with the situation, this could be a red flag for a person who takes on too much and doesn't follow through. The goal here is to look for winners.

- Stop and ask the candidate for questions. You have given the applicant quite a bit of content to think about, but the key is to see if he or she has been listening. A person who listens will have engaging questions relevant to the topics you presented. If the candidate asks questions about working hours or how the vacation plan works, kindly end the call. Remember to leave the door open to him or her sending questions afterward via e-mail. Eager people will follow up.

- Inform candidates of the process. A pet peeve of mine is leaving applicants hanging after an interview. Explaining the next steps in your hiring process is also helpful for you to set goals for yourself. For instance, tell candidates that you will come to a decision within two days about who to bring in for an in-person interview. This way, you don't drag out the interviewing process and you force yourself to make a decision.

Part 3
In-person interviewing

If a candidate has passed the phone interview and piqued your interest, bring him or her in quickly.

The follow-up discussion should follow a similar flow as the phone conversation. But this time around, you are really looking for how much information they retained from the first call.

Evangelizing your own product or service is one of the most important things you can do in an interview. The candidate needs to believe in you as much as they believe in the product.

The main goals of the in-person meeting are based around three simple questions: I reworded a few of the questions to highlight different aspects, but there are only three core attributes to look for.

- Would you enjoy spending eight hours a day with this person?
  —Is the candidate's energy similar to yours?
  —Is the candidate consistent with the details he or she gave you on the phone?
- Is this person capable of learning what you are teaching?
  —Do they listen well?
  —Do they ask relevant and timely questions?
- Can this person potentially teach you something?
  —Does the candidate have insight into the platform already?
  —How does he or she use the technology currently? Is that the same as your customers?
  —Does he or she willingly share information, or are they cagey about answers?

—Can the candidate clearly and, more important, concisely describe things?

If your answer is a resounding yes to all of the major questions above, the person may be a good hire. If you have an ounce of doubt, you may have to cut the person loose or come up with a training program to address your concerns.

Of course, you can spend more time grilling them on their resume, but, for the most part, a resume is not a very good reflection of a person's personality. Use the face-to-face time to check for a personality match.

Once again, when you are ending an in-person interview, inform the applicant what the process is moving forward. If you know right away that you don't want to hire the person, tell him or her as soon as possible.

Part 4
Test project

A test project is one of the most cost-effective ways of assessing a potential new hire before truly committing. The project must be relevant to the skill or technology that you are hiring for.

Some tips for a test project within technology:
- Make the project short so it can be done within an hour or so.
- Write out the instructions clearly. Leave out a few key details so the candidate has to ask questions. Part of the exercise for the applicant is to ask questions and not make assumptions.
- In the test description, make it clear that the candidate will need additional information to complete the assignment and that they will need to ask questions prior to starting.
- Put a due date on the project with a very specific time (e.g., Friday by 3:00 p.m.). If the candidate doesn't meet the deadline, your decision is easy. If the candidate delivers early, you know he or she is more eager than the average person. In my experience, around 20 percent of the people fail to deliver the project on time—or at all.
- • Ask the candidate to answer two or three questions about the assignment itself. For instance, what would you have done differently if you had to do this assignment again? Or, how would you rate your level of enthusiasm on this type of work on a scale of one to ten? Why?

Some good test projects to assess a variety of skills are:

- Explain X technology to your grandmother in five hundred words or less. Diagrams can be used instead of words.
- Explain three benefits of using X technology for my business that won't take more than an hour to implement.

- Explain why X technology is more important than TV in less than five hundred words.

These tasks are not testing the candidate's ability to practice a particular technology but are more focused on critical thinking and communication skills. A test project shows if the candidate truly understands how the technology interfaces with the rest of the world and if it is pertinent.

Part 5
A test relationship
Congratulations on making it to step 5! By this point, you have filtered out lots of people and are hopefully down to one or two candidates. It is time to make a choice and hire a new team member.

When entering into a new relationship, especially with younger workers, it is important to note that they are nervous about the relationship too.

The point of a test relationship is to allow both parties to get to know each other and provide an easy out if things don't work.

You can usually determine if a person is a good fit within a few days, but sometimes people take a little longer to warm up. I recommend setting up a one-month test period for each new employee.

How to make the most of our one-month test
Many employers use the thirty- or ninety-day test period to further vet employees. Most of the time, it goes horribly wrong because there is insufficient planning and a lack of mutual expectations.

A test-hire should be considered a totally blank canvas, even if they have industry experience. And even if they have industry experience, they don't have experience with your team or business processes. This is the stuff you want to focus on in the beginning.

Indoctrinating a new employee is largely skipped over for two main reasons: people are afraid of coming off as too overbearing, or they don't have time to train the new hire. Another reason is that people don't like the concept of "indoctrination," since it has a somewhat negative connotation.

The fact is, you have a business to run, and consistency is important to the customer.

To properly make use of a training period, it should be broken up into three main segments.

Training with expectations
In the training phase, focus on informing the new hire about the following:

- What the business does. Explain the big picture—what you sell, who your customers are, and how your customers buy what you sell.
- The goals of your business. This can be anything from customer service, profit, etc. The key is to make sure these statements are as detailed as possible. If you own a deli and your goal is to make the best sandwich in your town, define exactly what that means. For instance, explain that you use meats from organic farmers, locally grown lettuce, gluten-free bread, and homemade seasonal toppings and that you take an old-school approach to making a simple product to ensure it tastes great, is priced under $10, and the customer never has to wait more than five minutes to get it.

All of these details help to build a mental image for the new employee, which they can verify and then convey themselves to the customers. Even if a person is doing finance for you, they need to really believe in your product.

- Your customers and competitors. Ask the new hire to come in with fresh eyes and approach your product as a consumer would. This initial feedback helps not only to verify that your branding is correct, but it also provides free insight into problems regular customers may be seeing. Lastly, it helps the employee understand the product from the consumer perspective. At the end of this exercise, ask the new employee, "Would you buy from me or my competitor? Why?" Once again, you are trying to reinforce the belief in your product.

- Your product. If you have a physical product, let the new employee try to make and sell your product. Making sandwiches is full of tastes, smells, and textures, and requires a great level of consistency. This may, at times, be frustrating for employees who have been hired to do online marketing for you, but it is imperative that they understand how much care you put into your product. The connection to the five senses also helps build a much more robust brand image in their heads.

- Expectations. Educate the new employee on your personal expectations of them. Tell them what hours they need to be at work, how they need to dress, and what level of communication you want from them. Clearly spelling this out helps people know where the bar is and if they are meeting your expectations or falling short.

- Company processes. If your company has any specific processes around documents, communication, or HR, make sure those processes are well documented and communicated in the training phase. This shows structure in your company.

- Goals for the technical project.

- Test-period and training process. Let the new hire know about the test period process, the training phase, the projects, and the performance review. Tell new employees explicitly that you want them to put their best foot forward during this period. This simple statement usually nets a higher productivity since people know your expectations are high.

At this point, the new employee should have a fuller picture of how your business works and what you personally expect as a boss or manager.

To ensure you don't have to ad lib this procedure every time, take one to two hours to write down this process so anyone in your company can replicate it for a new hire.

Now that you have set the tone of what you want and how the system works, it is time to get your new teammate set up with an actual project.

Small, short projects
The small, short project phase is designed to mimic the instant gratification that most people get these days from games or social media.

Gamification is a relatively new term that describes how we are applying game thinking, game-design techniques, and game mechanics to everyday life. For example, if you give an employee a task to finish—say, a report—it is understood that this task is part of his or her duties. The gamified version of this would be that you ask them to finish the task within twenty-five minutes, and if they finish within twenty minutes, they get a bonus of a free coffee. The time parameters and prizes correlate to games and offer an incentive for regular duties. For the most part, younger generations respond well to these techniques, but the downside is that the rewards must be frequent and usually need to get larger over time to keep motivation high.

The longer the period between project completion and feedback, the less the feedback is heard or understood by the employee. Instant gratification is part of the overall gamification of our culture. Setting quick goals with very obvious rewards makes a project addictive. The rewards do not have to be monetary, by any means. The only thing that really matters is that there are more rewards available and the amount of rewards the person has earned is made somewhat public.

The projects that you want to create should be focused on developing core skills that can be used long-term in the job.

For example, if you need a person to be very good at time management, you may ask the person to measure the amount of time you spend on the phone versus with customers. The results of this tabulation should be presented in a clean and concise format with some written insights at the end.

A task like this doesn't take a lot of time to complete. The new employee learns how to observe and is forced to organize the results and reflect on the process itself at the end.

Coming up with suggestions on how to improve is usually quite hard to do, especially if you have been at a job for just one day.

The key to the short-term project is that you, as the manager, provide feedback at the end of the exercise. The feedback must be positive or constructive. Negative feedback will not work as effectively. When I say constructive, I mean the feedback must point out something that could be done better, and you need to actively work with the person to come up with a solution or show them a better way. This incorporates teaching into the relationship, which usually breeds respect from the employee. We are taught from an early age to respect our teachers. Conversely, we are usually taught to hate our bosses. The choice here is pretty obvious.

In terms of feedback, incorporating frequent and quick rewards is key to boosting the new employee's morale and confidence. Rewards can come in the form of a simple compliment, such as, "Great job. You not only got this done really fast, but you really asked good questions along the way. Keep up the communication skills!"

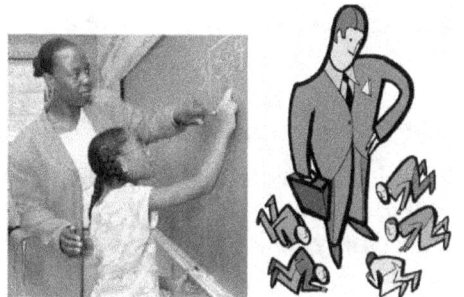
Exhibit 31 - Teacher or Boss? Which will you be?

All employees will need more than kind words to keep their motivation high. Offering financial rewards or gifts as prizes is a great way to keep things moving along. At first, business owners have the urge to put together big gifts, like a vacation for four to Hawaii. There are several issues with this from the small business owner perspective. A trip for four is expensive. You may not be able to afford to give this away often. It takes a long time to win something so big, once again reducing the overall effect.

Focusing on small, frequent gifts is cost-effective for you and appreciated by employees. For example, $10–50 gift cards can be given away quite often. If the average trip for four people to Hawaii is $10,000, you can potentially give away two hundred $50 gift cards for that same $10K. The other side of this is lottery mentality; people think they have a better chance of winning when there are more prizes.

Having two hundred units of praise and reward is quite powerful.

Part 6
Reviewing
Reviews are something that most companies don't do very well because most managers don't have a good review process. If you do not know how to conduct a review, the employee is certainly not going to tell you how to do it.

Everyone has a different process for reviews. Some are more formal, while others are more casual. Even though the review can be quite time-intensive, it is a very valuable time investment. This conversation is really one-on-one time.

Start with a goal for the review. Do you want to hire this person full-time? Do you want to promote them? Do you want to fire them? Do you want to give them a raise?

This goal should be set at the beginning of the review period. For instance, if you conduct quarterly reviews and the quarter begins on January 1, set the goal at that time. Tell the employee that at the end of the trial period he or she will be given a formal review that will determine if he or she is hired full-time.

Part 7
Hire or fire?

In the past thirty days, you have worked hard to find a gem of an employee. Keep in mind that hiring is never an exact science; it is OK to make a mistake and need to let a new hire go.

If you have to fire the person and you know this quite soon into the testing period, cut them loose quickly. If you keep the person around too long, they will turn into a virus, infecting your other employees with bad morale, or your other employees will team up against this person, creating unnecessary politics in the workplace.

If you do decide to hire the employee for the long term, it is good to revise your goals for this person, reiterate his or her duties, and formally bestow the new staffer with a title. This affirmation is a great way of saying, "We are now in an official relationship. Welcome to the team."

After you hire the employee, things to focus on are really rooted in the review and the reward process.

Make time to be a good manager, and remember, people don't manage themselves.

Summary:

Part 1 – Review the resumes – use broad strokes
Part 2 – Set up a screening call to probe into their resume
Part 3 – Set up an in person interview and spend this time to assess the cultural fit
Part 4 – Get them a test project – Don't make it too hard, and create an opportunity for them to wow you.
Part 5 – Test Relationship – Set up expectations and make sure communication lines are open for feedback.

Part 6 – Reviewing – Always set up time to reflect by providing critical, correctional and supportive feedback.

Part 7 – Cut your losses early if it is was a bad hire, and reward the people who are trying extra hard.

Creating a process for onboarding a new team member may be a lengthy process but it really helps keep things structured as your company grows. It also openly sets expectations, which usually give people something to aim for.

Chapter 18 - Differences between Tech and Design Teams

Our greatest strength as a human race is our ability to acknowledge our differences,
our weakness is our failure to embrace them.
—Judith Henderson

Tech and design teams tend to differ quite a bit in terms of personality. The main thing to remember is that both teams are eager to help you and build a great product, but each may require a slightly different communication approach.

Tips for working with design teams

A design team will include designers and copywriters. The designers will work on all your graphics, the layout, and the general user experience on your site. The copywriter will be responsible for writing the text on your site. Sometimes this is the same person.

The creative team needs to know:
- The main features of the site.
- Who the tech person is.
- Your brand standards.
- Who your customers are.

These basic pieces of information, which are usually incorporated into the RFP, will greatly help guide the creative team. One issue I have run into is that the RFP is read and answered by the business person on the team but never actually gets relayed to the creative team. Make sure you hold a kickoff meeting to get everyone on the same page.

Things that really irritate creative teams:
- Micromanaging is usually something that will drive your creative team nuts.
- Not trusting your team to deliver solid results. If for some reason you don't agree on a direction, as the client, you have every right to voice your concerns and opinion. But be prepared to deal with a person who might stop working on your project, leaving you high and dry.
- Not providing enough direction or changing your mind too often. Providing copious amounts of information *before* the project starts is a good way to avoid confusion later. It also creates a written reference point to work from later on.

- As a client, you must also be conscious about changing direction with the design team. Keep in mind the creative team usually bills by the hour, so every time you make a larger change in direction this potentially cuts into your budget.

- Providing critical comments but no praise. People like to hear good things once in a while. Remember to give praise when it is due. If you just dole out the negative news, you will end up with a team member who won't want to work with you again. Keep in mind you may need more creative work in the future, and having a reliable resource is going to be key. Don't burn your bridges!

For the most part, the same rules apply for your tech team. The only difference that I find quite apparent is that engineers can be a bit more literal and need very specific direction. Leaving things up for interpretation is a great way to waste time and creates something you don't want.

Documentation is key with the tech team; make sure you have detailed your project as well as possible. And make sure your tech team can access you at any time for questions. Lastly, encourage the questions. It is better to ask questions versus building something and then having to redo it. A strong web firm will take time to get the requirements down before quoting the price. They will also take time to check in at specific milestones to make sure the project is going in the right direction.

Summary

Trust your team's skill; that is why you hired them. Provide as much detail as you can. Encourage questions and dialogue during the process.

Chapter 19 - The Kickoff Meeting

There are only two mistakes one can make along the road to truth; not going all the way, and not starting - Buddha

The kickoff meeting is a relatively short meeting to start a project. The intent is to get everyone on the same page and make sure everyone has access to the same information.

As mentioned earlier, the RFP may not make it to all people within the team. It is your job as the client to make sure that everyone knows what your goals are.

Components of a successful kickoff meeting:
- Restate the project.
- State the goals of the project.
- Define who the customer is and show examples, if possible.
- Show examples of a competitor's technology.
- Define the deadlines.
- Define who is on the team and their roles.
- Walk the team through major use case scenarios with competitor sites or with wireframes.

Wireframe resources
For example wireframes, I suggest the following websites:

Mockingbird
https://gomockingbird.com/
This is an online tool to make wireframes. It is easy to use and free for one project.

Balsamiq
www.balsamiq.com
Another online tool that allows you to wireframe for desktops and mobile devices. Also has a helpful tutorial.

About.com
http://graphicdesign.about.com/od/effectivewebsites/ss/wireframes.htm
A useful, albeit a bit dated, tutorial. The basic principles remain the same.

A well-run kickoff meeting is a great way to set the tone of the project and get everyone focused on the same goal.

Dedicating one to two hours to a high-quality kickoff meeting can yield massive benefits for project efficiency.

Summary

Get everyone together to start the project. Be clear with direction. Make information accessible to everyone on the team. Leave the door open for questions.

Chapter 20 - Engaging a Team

I hope if dogs take over the world, and they choose a king, they just don't go by size, because I bet there are some Chihuahuas with some good ideas.
—Jack Handy

When choosing an agency or web developer to help you, there are a few tactics you can use to mitigate your risk.

The single most important thing to remember here is that you always need to have a written contract before starting work. Do not under any circumstance engage a web firm or developer with just a verbal or e-mail confirmation.

The written contract should cover, at minimum, the following:
- Exactly what will be built, detailing look and feel, technology, etc.
- Process of how the teams will work together and the steps involved.
- Timeline and/or milestones.
- Estimated cost.
- Information on post-project maintenance costs.
- Physical address of the vendor with phone and e-mail.
- Designation of which state will govern the agreement.
- Cancellation or refund clauses.
- Billing method, whether hourly or on a project basis.
- Payment methods, whether check, wire transfer, credit card, or barter.
- What the actual deliverables will be.
- Creative asset rights and costs.
- External References

Before we go any further, there are some differences between a web agency and a web developer. The sample contracts here can be used for both a developer and agency. Most of the time an agency is slightly larger or offers more services than just basic web development. A web developer may be a group of people but is often one person that is directly developing for you. In some cases the agency may have a contract of their own, that you may want to vet against the recommendations here.

Finances
Always ask the agency or web development firm to put together a clear description of the costs coordinated to the overall scope of work and timeline.

The standard in the industry is to pay a deposit of 10 to 25 percent up front, and then pay the remainder over the course of the project as various milestones are hit. The benefits of this method are that you are incentivizing the team to hit its deadlines and you are paying for results, not just time.

I strongly recommend against paying hourly for any folks taking on a tech or creative project for the first time, especially with a person you have never done business with. The vast majority of freelancers don't use accurate time management tools. This means you could be paying for the person to research, sit around while something updates, etc.

If the team insists on billing by the hour, then as the client you have the following rights:

- The right to audit the team's work at any given time by simply asking, "What have you guys done today and how long did it take?" You also have the right to ask this as often as you want. Is it annoying? Perhaps, but it is your money.
- The right to ask the team to use a time management tool to create online records that you can review every day.
- The right to ask for billing based either on fifteen-minute blocks or by the minute. If a person says, "I bill by the hour, and I round up," be careful with this arrangement. That means they can work twenty-five minutes and charge you for a full hour.
- The right to a weekly report indicating whether the project is moving as originally projected or taking longer. For instance, if the vendor projects fifty hours of work over two weeks and spends forty-five hours in week one, there is a chance the vendor might go over budget and over time.

If you are being forced to pay hourly, I recommend asking for a few safeguards. For example, if the project is projected to take fifty hours of work, it may be reasonable to request that if the project exceeds fifty-five hours, the agency agrees to either absorb the overtime or charge a lower rate, since the original estimation was more than 10 percent off.

On the flip side, make sure your billing agreement is based on actual hours instead of the max projection. If the team quoted you fifty hours and they only use forty, you should only pay for forty hours of work. This rarely happens, but it is something to include in the contract nonetheless.

Contract termination best practices

Even if you do your best with due diligence, there are times when things won't work out. Including a clause about contract termination is recommended to help you define what will happen if the two parties decide to split.

This clause simply states what you as the client will have to pay and what the vendor will have to deliver if there is a mutually agreed-upon split. From personal experience, the worst thing that happens is your developer doesn't work out and doesn't deliver you the final code after taking your money. Using an escrow service, offered by sites like Elance and oDesk, can provide substantial protection in cases like this. The escrow works like a third-party bank account. Every time the developer hits a milestone successfully, a payment is released. If for some reason there is a dispute, sites like Elance and oDesk may help with resolving the issue as an unbiased third party.

Deliverables
In the contract, make sure there is a clear definition of what you will actually get at the end of the project. With virtual products like a website, you may want to state that you get all log-in information and a backup copy of the site with all modifications or custom code included. When you wrap up the project, you can use this checklist to confirm that you are receiving exactly what you paid for.

Creative assets
When it comes to creative assets like copy, images, and video, you need to consider copyright law. The contract should clearly state who owns the creative rights to the copy, images, video, and even code. Usually, this can be solved with language such as "all copyrights will be owned by the client after final payment is made." It should also be clearly explained that the vendor may not reuse code or creative assets for another client without your express permission.

In regard to paying for stock photos, videos, or other creative assets, sometimes creative vendors will include this in their cost, other times they will ask the client to pay for each asset.

Process
When creating the contract, it is extremely important to detail what steps are included.

For instance, some web agencies may only say that the design and coding is included. This can sometimes lead to confusion about inclusion of other components, such as QA or an initial consultation.

I usually recommend that each contract cover the following topics at minimum.
- Initial consultation where the project is defined and a complete scope of work is created. This period is also helpful to field any questions.
- Architecture.
- Coding.
- Design.
- Quality assurance.
- Bug-fixing.
- Transfer of the actual technology or rights to you.

Making sure all of these topics are covered helps protect your interests as the client and helps clarify the relationship to the vendor.

External material references
All of the external documents—materials like graphics, details about the project, etc.—that have already been delivered should be properly referenced in the contract. This

helps centralize all communication and creates a much stronger reference document if there is a future dispute or disagreement.

You can even cut and paste these documents to the end of the contract as appendices.

Since I am not a lawyer, I think it is better to reference a contract than to write one myself. The following two contracts are very well respected in the industry and cover the most important topics. The first template even allows you to choose alternatives or options that best suit your needs. The second contract is written in more layperson's terms and may work for smaller engagements, but I would use it with caution for higher-priced arrangements.

Template 1
Shawn Adrian of Nerdburn.com.
http://blog.nerdburn.com/entries/tips-for-freelancers/sample-web-design-contract-budget-timeline-proposal

Template 2.
Andy Clarke of 24ways.org.
http://24ways.org/2008/contract-killer

Summary

Always put an agreement together to formalize the arrangement. This agreement should be as comprehensive as possible, especially where covering the definition of the project, costs, timelines, and the rights of each party.

Section III – Measure

In section III I would like to focus on getting you to look backwards. At this point, I hope you have developed a better picture of where you are, and where you want to go as a small business. The most reliable way for you to tell if you are progressing is to look at what success or failures you have had.

Measuring your progress is a great way to see if you are spending your time and money in the right places. This is a two facet approach, it involves checking your goals from your point of view and from your customer's point of view.

Chapter 21 - Monitoring Your Team & Customer

As soon as the boss decides he wants his workers to do something, he has two problems, making them do it and monitoring what they do.
—Robert Krulwich

By now, you are a seasoned pro in terms of defining a project, defining goals, and finding a team to execute those goals.

The next step in your project is making sure things run smoothly.

There are two main ways of doing this. The first method is for slightly larger teams, which involves working with a dedicated product or project manager.

The project manager is the person who is responsible for several key tasks.

First, the project manager should set up a strong foundation by implementing standards and defining the tools. The standards might be that the team assembles every Tuesday at 9:00 a.m. for a status meeting and that certain people get CCed on various topics. Regarding tools, the manager may set up online calendars, central document storage, check-in/check-out processes, bug trackers, timelines, milestones, and task management systems.

These foundational elements help reduce friction when it comes to communication and ensure everyone is kept in the loop. The tools create a way of literally measuring progress and costs.

In many web agencies, a project manager may overlap with the account manager or business development person. Sometimes this is good; sometimes it is bad. The only thing you need to worry about is if this person is hitting your milestones and providing insight that you may need into the project.

For smaller organizations and projects, I recommend a somewhat simpler solution.

As the client, since your core concern is about getting the project out the door, you really need to manage just two key factors: time and quality.

Regarding time, the single most effective way to manage the project is to mark your calendar to call or e-mail the team every week or at every milestone. Usually, if you just ask, "Is everything on schedule?" teams will invariably answer, "Yes." Ask a vague question, get a vague answer.

Phone calls are usually more efficient and can easily be followed up with an e-mail.

If milestones were defined by the web agency or developer, then there should already be a simple checklist of things that should be done at each milestone. Take the time to go through each milestone and see if it has been completed, if there were any issues, and if the team has questions.

If the milestone has not been completed, you need to find out two things: what is holding it back and what will be delayed because of it.

Oftentimes during these status meetings, if it's determined a feature will be delayed, the meeting will get stalled talking about it. Be cautious about using all of your team's time for something that can be discussed in a more private setting. Also, stay focused on completing the agenda items on time. This way, everything gets covered well during the meeting and the team overall can keep moving forward.

No matter how you handle an issue, the most important thing you can do at the end of the meeting is make sure that someone on the team is responsible for following up or closing the issue. If no one is assigned responsibility, it will never get finished.

When running a smaller project, it is important to keep quality standards high. Quality is a somewhat vague metric, since it can mean different things to different people. The way I recommend getting your team rallied around quality is to ask them during your various milestone conferences a simple question: "Is this technology meeting our original customer goals?" If the technology is meeting the goal, but in a roundabout way you are potentially lowering quality by making it harder for the consumer to interact with your business. Keep things simple, and remind your team of the consumer goals often.

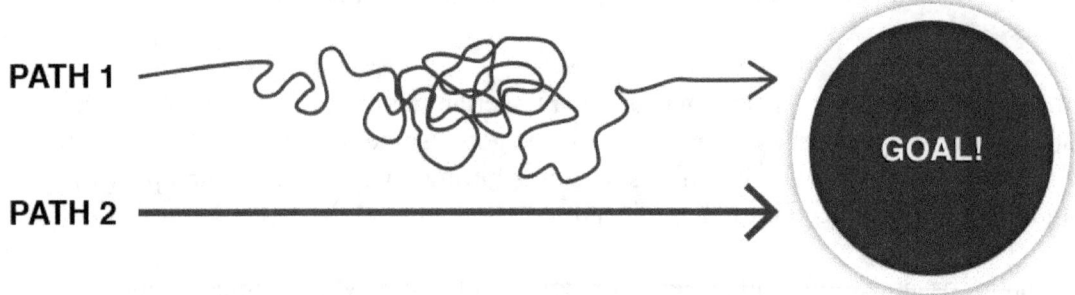

Exhibit 32. A direct path is always better. Keep it short and simple.

Your path to a goal should be clear and direct. Making a process complicated or long is a great way to lower sales and frustrate customers.

Summary

Create checkpoints for your project. Remind your team of the goals. Make sure communication within the team is efficient.

Chapter 22 - Turning Your Tech into Revenue or Cost Savings

Leaders must invoke an alchemy of great vision. -Henry A. Kissinger

One of the core principles of this book is that every tech project you take on should have a measurable and actionable metric behind it.

I always like to start with projects that can be measured with revenue or customer growth. This ensures the investment of time and money has a very specific dollar return.

The other way to look at tech projects is to see how much money they might potentially save you.

Each project will vary quite a bit, so what we will try to do here is lay out a framework for creating your own metric.

Measurement framework

1. Restate your project's goal.
Make sure the original reason you designed this feature or tech project is still valid. For example, let's say you just wanted to reduce the number of calls about your hours of operation. The goal here would be to make it easier to find your hours of operation on your website and potentially add it to your Google Places page.

2. Restate the metric.
Continuing with the example, let's say you wanted to reduce phone calls by 50 percent. Currently, you average twenty calls per week asking about the hours of operation.

3. Determine how you can gather that data and make it easy to repeat.
In this particular scenario, you don't need any fancy tools, just a notebook and pen to mark down every time a person calls about the hours of operation. Create a column for week one without the new feature and another for week two with the new feature.

4. Determine if you are going to give the feature some more love or a correction.
Let's say you find that you reduced the number of calls in week two to five calls. This beat your goal of a 50 percent reduction with a 75 percent reduction in calls.

Given that the results were quite strong, you decide to not invest any more into this feature and consider it a success. The reason behind this is that you may never be able to get to zero calls, and the amount of effort required to eliminate the last five calls may not be worth the cost.

For a moment, let's say you only reduced the number of calls by two, so you were still getting eighteen calls a week. This didn't meet your goal, but the good news is that you have a few options to fix it.

You can either give it a bit more time to see if it gradually decreases, or you can do some more testing.

The No vs. Huh responses

To make sure your new testing is as low-cost as possible, you should ask each consumer who calls in, "Did you happen to see our new feature on our website?" If the answer is, "No, I couldn't find it," then you know it wasn't executed well. If the answer is, "No, I didn't even look," then we know our customers are not in the same place as our feature. This is an important insight since it indicates that we may not have done our initial customer research correctly. We could have saved time and money by just asking our customers (for free) if they use our website to find basic info or if they prefer to call. If your customer base is traditionally much older, they may prefer to call, while if your audience is younger, you may see that most use a computer or mobile device to find relevant information.

5. Set a deadline or timeline for the next check-in. If you only check stats once, you may never be sure if they are getting better, worse, or staying stable.

One of the issues I see with companies starting to analyze or measure things is that they have trouble making it part of their weekly or monthly routine. All you have to do is make a calendar reminder of when you should check your stats again. Simple, cheap, and it gets you into a routine or process of caring about measurement.

Summary

Measuring your success is almost as important as the success itself.

Chapter 23 - Reflecting on Your Decisions

There are three principal means of acquiring knowledge...observation of nature, reflection, and experimentation. Observation collects facts; reflection combines them; experimentation verifies the result of that combination.
—Denis Diederot

Life moves fast. There is no way around this. But the greatest thing is that we can hit pause and take a moment to reflect on whether we've met our goals, if our goals are the right ones, and if we want to continue down this route or change course.

I strongly recommend taking a moment at the end of each month to review your technology decisions by asking the following questions.

If the project is still ongoing:
- What is holding the project back, or is it running on time?
- Is my timeline still reasonable?
- Is the consumer need still there, or has it changed?
- Am I on budget?
- Do I need help on any particular part?

For completed projects:
- Regarding the overall decision
  — Did it matter that I wasn't an early adopter? If yes, what was the monetary loss?
- Regarding organization
  —Did I stick to my deadline?
  —Did I have insight into the project when it was going on?
  —Did I allocate enough time to respond to the team's needs?
  —Was I realistic with the deadline?
- Regarding finances
  —Did I stick to my budget?
  —Was my original budget sufficient?
  —Am I happy with the quality given the cost? If not, why not?
- Regarding communication
  —Did the team communicate well? If not, what could have been better?
  —Did I provide any positive feedback during the process?
  —Did I change my mind during the process? If so, why? Were my goals realistic?
- Regarding customers
  —Have I asked my customers about the new tech? Do they like it, or do they have any suggestions?

—Has the new tech driven any revenue? Is this revenue in addition to regular sales?
- Regarding the new tech
  —Do I feel comfortable with the technology? Do I need more training?
  —Do I know how to get hold of a person if something is broken?
  —Am I checking it to see if it is broken?
  —Are there any major errors? If so,
    • What is the plan for getting them fixed?
    • What is the deadline?
    • What are the costs?
- Regarding future tech
  —What should I add next?
  —When should I take on a new project?
  —How much should I budget this time around?
  —Will I use the same team?
  —Would I recommend the team to a friend?

All of these questions do not have to be answered, but if this is your first tech project, it is a good way to see if you want to do this again or hire in-house help to take care of this in the future. It is also a good way to evaluate your decision-making skills coupled with your ability to follow through on a project.

Most companies will call this the postmortem process, since you are looking at a project after it is completed. Many companies don't allocate any time for this process, as they are moving too fast. These companies typically suffer from systemic management issues that can usually be solved. The downside of this is that no one with decision-making authority is taking the time to define the issue and find a solution for it.

The postmortem process can be done electronically, but it usually goes a bit faster if you just gather everyone from the project in a room and talk about the project with the guide above.

Summary
Make time to reflect by yourself and with your team. Use what you learn to guide future projects.

Chapter 24 - What Could Go Wrong?

With any methodology, there is always something that can go wrong. A lot of this is chalked up to human error or people not following the methodology to a T.

For instance, if you have ever heard Eric Ries, author of *The Lean Startup*, speak, you will hear rumblings in the crowd about how his method doesn't work or is unrealistic. I think Eric's response to those comments would be something like, "The methodology is a fundamental change to your organization and not just something you try out for a short period of time."

The change affects your communication and core processes and your perception of costs, time, and perfection. The whole way we do business has to shift; we need to get everyone in the organization on the same page to really make these things work. There are even cases when we need to get external partners to update their processes to get things moving more efficiently. The focus doesn't have to be speed all the time. Efficiency may manifest as a cost savings or being able to gain feedback with the least amount of input.

So if you decide to implement any new process within your business, your core task outside of the project itself is making sure everyone on the team is fully on board and aware of what is going on.

Will there be issues or hiccups the first few times around? Yes, this is almost guaranteed. But you don't have to worry about these issues unless you ignore the education that comes along with them. If you consistently try new things and never take a moment to learn from your mistakes, the process itself is fruitless.

Throughout each chapter of this book, my goal has been to highlight certain things that are easy to get wrong. The vast majority of what can go wrong usually boils down to two main issues: poor communication and poor time management.

Will you realistically be able to turn yourself into an amazing communicator or time manager overnight? Probably not. You don't have to be perfect at these things, just aware of your actions and how they might be impacting others on your team.

Every once in a while, check in with yourself and ask, "Am I the bottleneck?" If the answer is yes, it is time to either delegate some duties or slow down the project.

Chapter 25 - It Is Going to Be OK—You Are Not Alone

Out of intense complexities intense simplicities emerge. —Winston Churchill

Small business and technology are essentially strangers passing in the night. Each one needs the other, but there are so many other things going on every day, it is hard to stop to see if there is a fit.

Letting some technology pass you by is OK; ignoring obvious signals is not.

A ton of new technology will always present itself. It is not your job to test and verify each new thing that comes out. Please remember that!

Listening to your core customers is the best way to filter what technologies you should be paying attention to. These are your obvious signals. The signals usually start off quietly and infrequently, but as the technology grows and becomes mainstream, the signals become louder and more frequent. You don't pay attention to the ambulance five miles away that you can barely hear; you pay attention to the ambulance blaring right next to you.

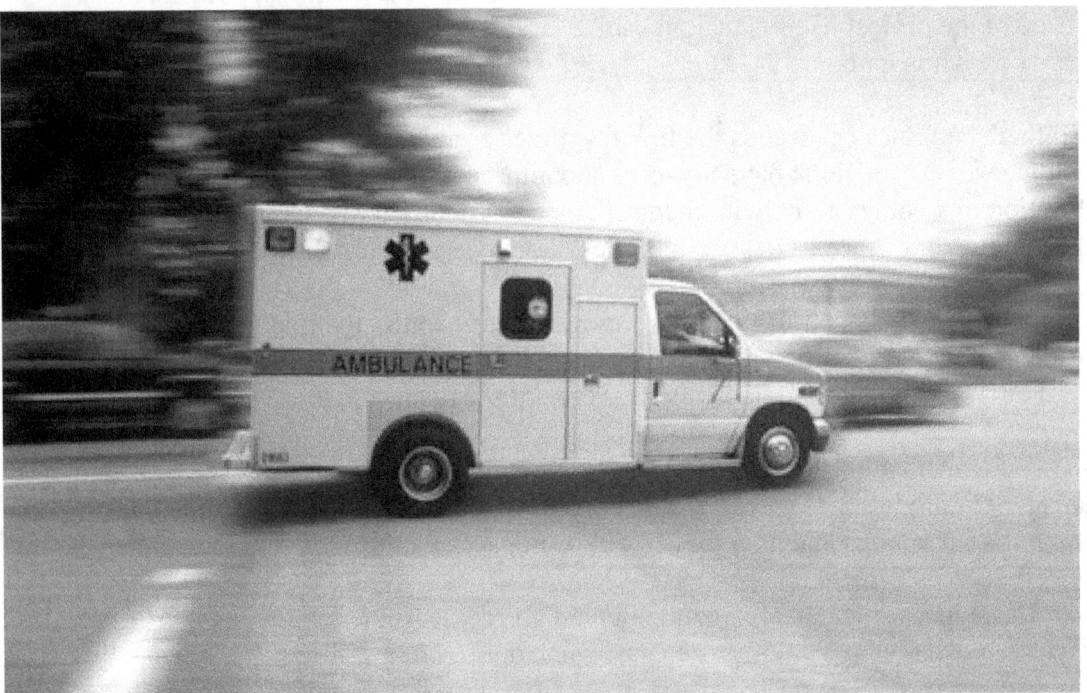

Exhibit 33. The ambulance is coming—are you listening?

That is when you have to consciously and quickly make a decision. If you ignore these free and loud signals, you are missing out on valuable feedback for your company.

There will be instances when you really want to try out the new technology, but it will not make financial sense for your business. If you can't see how the technology might help you drive more customers or revenue or lower costs, that is OK. Asking well-qualified and poignant questions of other business owners will help you determine if this technology is relevant to your business specifically.

As a small business, your time is very valuable and so is your money. Always look for the least risky way of testing a new technology. Most of the time, you can verify or eliminate an idea by just asking questions, which are always free.

With this book, my three main goals are the following:

- You become stronger at choosing technology that is relevant, measurable, and related to a business goal.
- You find the book helpful, and you decide to wait on investing in new technology.
- You feel reassured that everything is not urgent, and you pass along the book to fellow business owners to help them save time and money too.

Don't ever underestimate the value of the customer standing right in front of you. As a brick and mortar business, you have the ultimate luxury of being able to talk to your customer at any point in time.

Take advantage of simplicity every day. Good luck.

Appendix

Prospective Technology Checklist

Use this simple chart to compare technologies you might be interested in testing. You can compare Facebook versus Twitter or TV versus radio.

The point of this exercise is to make sure the technology is something that is relevant to your business.

	TV	Print	Social	Web
Do my customers use it?				
Is this a Fad? (Are the majority of my customers using it?)				
Are other businesses seeing revenue/success there?				
Can I connect it to revenue?				
Can I measure it? What is the metric?				
How much will it cost?				
How much time will it take?				
Can I maintain it?				
Can I delegate this?				
Will it hurt me if I don't do this now?				
Is there a way of simplifying it to test it?				

- Web design
    —Firms and websites

- Social media pages as news outlets
    •—Make Google+ and Facebook pages

- Social media tutorials

- Other books to read
    —*The Lean Startup: How Today's Entrepreneurs Use Continuous Innovation to Create Radically Successful Businesses* by Eric Ries. Great book about how to keep your business methodology focused on efficient learning rather than long-term, large-scale projects. http://www.amazon.com/The-Lean-Startup-Entrepreneurs-Continuous/dp/0307887898/ref=sr_1_1?ie=UTF8&qid=1339097300&sr=8-1
    —*The E Myth: Why Most Businesses Don't Work and What to Do About It* by Michael E. Gerber. Excellent book about how to be an effective small business entrepreneur.
    —*Blink: The Power of Thinking Without Thinking* by Malcolm Gladwell. Focuses on simplicity and listening to gut reactions as key decision drivers.

- Online classes
    —Udemy?

- Online cost management tools—apps to tell you how much you make.

- List of engineers for apps, web apps, websites, etc.

- Sample sites and why they look good.

www.ingramcontent.com/pod-product-compliance
Lightning Source LLC
Chambersburg PA
CBHW081454170526
45166CB00008B/2431